Martin Nicholas Kunz

best | designed

wellness hotels

NORTH AND SOUTH AMERICA . CARIBBEAN . MEXICO

avedition lebensart

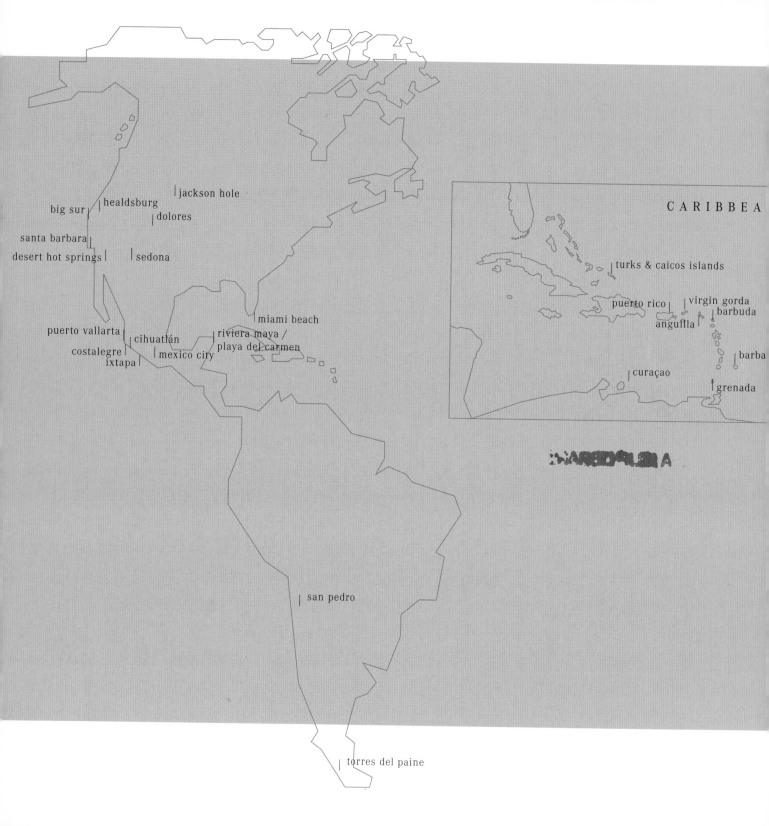

jackson hole

big sur | healdsburg
| dolores

santa barbara
desert hot springs | | sedona

miami beach

puerto vallarta
| cihuatlán | riviera maya /
costalegre | | playa del carmen
ixtapa | | mexico city

C A R I B B E A

| turks & caicos islands

puerto rico | | virgin gorda
| barbuda
anguilla

| barba

| curaçao
| grenada

san pedro

| torres del paine

One could catagorize all the hotels displayed over the next 168 pages by saying that they're simply beautiful. Easy.

One could let the photos do the talking and begin to dream, imagine what it would be like, lying on a teak lounger, sunken into the warm sand of a beach, rippling ocean and lightly tumbling waves in the background. Or how about the sea's mineral-scented spray, meditation in the comfortable shade of magnificent palms, or the simple pleasure of two trained hands pushing the stress out of tensed-up shoulders? It's enough to make you rush out and book the flights, or at least start looking for them on the internet.

These properties awaken longing, but also expectations.

The pictures you'll see here add to those expectations, and are part of a certain staging the hotels allow themselves to be part of. They are the result of the subjective view of a photographer and the compositional skill of a graphic designer, deliberately appealling to the emotions.

But each of the hotels here also has a particular story to tell; has its own spirit. A special element, light-years away from the average, profit-driven, drawing-board planning of a souless, functional product. The properties here have personalities behind them; people that have transferred their own philosophies into a concrete form. An illustrious group encompassing hard-nosed businesspeople looking for competitive superiority, and

burned-out managers seeking a chance for contemplation. Talented adventurers, building their own alternative worlds; opting out, but actually embarking on a third or fourth career as hotelier. Among this group are investors, wanting to see their money grow in the middle of the jungle, or rich heirs, driven by an idea and a sense of aethstetic value that becomes an obsession.

The results, as one would expect, are unique. Each has its own advantages, as well as its individual drawbacks. We want to tell you about both, and above all, about the details that you can't see in the photos; about the people that are standing to the side, out of shot. We'll include the food you can't taste, the aroma of the plants you can't smell, the sounds you can't hear, the –

sometimes eventful – journeys that led us to these places, and the wellness experiences that you can't feel.

We want to report on the amazing successes, but also give an insight to the breaks in style, inconsequent details, bad lighting, hasty construction decisions and bathrooms that just don't work. Dog-earred rugs, mosquito attacks and

sleepless nights don't show up in carefully arranged images, but they could all play a significant role in affecting the realization of the fantasies and expectations of travelers before they arrive.

Late afternoon. The Mexicana Fokker 100 curves its way past the kilometer-high towers of cloud, which dissolve towards the earth into fog and

rain. Through breaks in the gray, an endless, lumpy bushland with thousands of undeveloped Maya towns. Further ahead lies Yucatan, in bright sunshine, its coast appearing as if drawn by a shaky hand. A couple more stomach-lurching punches from the side-winds, and the aircraft lands. Cancun: a brash showcase of industrial-size hotels and casinos full of slots; a Garden of Eden for the American tourist masses.

Then something really strange happens. The first baggage on the conveyor is ours, which is good news for Betsy, with her daughter and friend, just arrived from Los Angeles. They've just climbed into the van that's taking us to Deseo, and haven't had to wait long. After a hearty welcome, we make our way along the fast road to Playa del Carmen; meanwhile the most popular party destination south of Ibiza. A mental introduction follows with an ambient relaxation cassette, that the driver starts with a flourish. No, the hotel isn't on the beach, he comments, as Betsy's daughter, Jennifer, is busy thinking about jumping through the waves. It's on Fifth Avenue, right in the center, where everything's going on.

"Yeah, Deseo's cool. You'll love it", yodels our friendly chauffeur from behind the wheel. Betsy and her travelling companions are exhausted after their five-hour flight from the US west coast. They discovered the hotel in the magazine "Travel + Leisure". "Fantastic architecture...love the daybeds and the fabric shades. Looks great, huh?".

Now close this book and look at the cover.

It's true; the image releases your imagination, doesn't it? Between the wafting swathes of linen lies inspiration, freedom and regeneration. The architecture of the young Mexican team "Central de Arquitectura" is sensational. This forward thinking group has created a modern milestone, spiced with unusual traditional flavors. What "Travel + Leisure" didn't tell Betsy was that the small 15-room building is in the epicenter of the nightlife district,

and is indeed one of the area's hottest spots. It's not for nothing that Deseo's concept is entitled "Hotel + Lounge".

In fact, it might make even more sense to put "lounge" first. The core of the property is the bar on the fabulous f irst-floor terrace, with those tempting daybeds. Approached via Mayan temple-styled stone steps, guests throw themselves into the throng of party-people, or kick-back on one of the couches between the pool and guestrooms. With video projections on the walls,

generously mixed cocktails and the latest lounge tunes, the scene is complete. There's massage, a chilled-out breakfast buffet of fresh fruit and tropical juices, tapas at night and DJ's. Wellness here has more to do with decadent ease, and fitness means fit to party. Not much chance for Betsy to get some peace and quiet, or for Jennifer to build sandcastles though...

In contrast, complete peace and quiet, and the soothing rush of the sea can be enjoyed without limit at Cap Juluca on

Anguilla. Feet up and absorb the views of St. Maarten. Directly behind the gold and turquoise beach landscape, screened by a band of lush green, the resort's intensely white villas are strung along the coast like pearls. An architectural composition with noble, Moorish elements. Terracotta steps and arcades, towers that mirror ancient citadels, domes, balconies, courtyards and always the luminescent Andalusian bright white. For photographers, a dream job, full of spectacular motifs and enticing vistas.

But open the door to Cap Juluca's interior, and the story is very, very different. A traditional, clubroom feel, with shades of brown, heavy armchairs and a touch of bourgeois reserve. The harmony and elegance of the exterior is certainly a contrast to the occasionally ostentatious décor inside. What remains constant, however, is the atmosphere. Exclusive, but laid-back.

Stunning design and peace can be found together on Mexico's west coast. On the

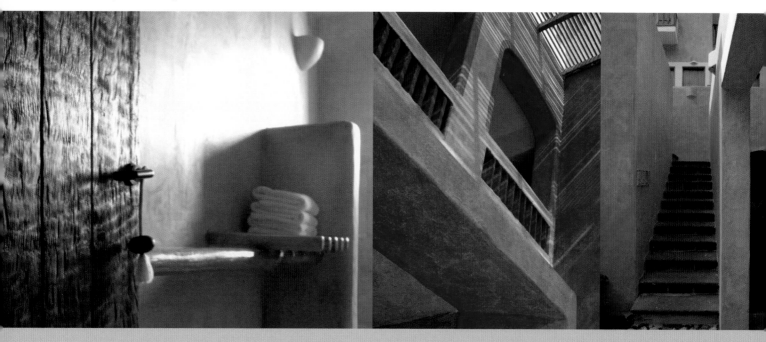

Costalegre sits an architectonic paradise, brought to life by the passion and vision of one former banker. Gian Franco Brignone made his way to Mexico at the end of the 70s. In Paris, the Italian threw in the towel on his lucrative job, and exchanged a slice of his fortune for several hundred acres of coastland, complete with tropical forest, deserted bays and rocky coves. His plan: to realize a personal fantasy of a better, more beautiful world. Together with his architects, Marco Aldaco, Diego Villaseñor and Jean Claude Galibert, he started constructing their designs by the dozen; luxury villas that would not look out of place at an international trade fair or Expo. Majestic constructions that respect their natural location, perched on hills above the ocean, slipped in between thick forest. They take the beauty of the landscape, capture it and create powerful images from it. On every corner, through every window, through each door is a new composition. From the bed, from the terrace and even from the shower, the scene is set. So where's the snag?

Perhaps the place is too remote, although that's probably more of an advantage than anything else. No, the catch here is money. Those that wish to experience this wonder are going to need plenty of it. Split the cost with a few friends, and the outcome is very acceptable…but then you have to go with friends, and the bay below your villa is no longer yours. The silent expanse of wilderness you command from your balcony suddenly has three or four other kings and queens to rule over it too. It's just not the same.

One could continue to talk about positive and negative, about surprises, good and bad. The oil platforms before the Bacara Resort, for example, and its fascinating avocado plantations; or the incredibly friendly atmosphere at Rhoni and Cristina's Sagewater Spa.

Then there are the rooms at Enchantment Resort, which aren't always 100% consistent, but are made up for by the striking design at Mi amo Spa, and its wondrous panoramas of Sedona's fire-red cliffs. We could mention the rustic

attraction of Christoph Henkel and Bernd Kuhlmann's Dunton Hot Springs, the refined, champers-slurping clientele of the Amangani, the trimmed colonial cool at Parrot Cay, or the tequila-filled waterpistols at the Water Club. Then there's the plunge-pool on the first floor of the Villa del Sol beach suite, the roof-top bar at Habita, the spa whirlpool at Ikal del Mar, surrounded by candles, the "no electicity" philosophy at Hotelito Desconocido and the window-framed views of the Torres del Paine peaks at explora en Patagonia...

But we don't want to give it all away now. There are a few more pages to flick through first. And at the end, what really counts are the personal experiences. Visit these places for yourself, and paint your own pictures of them. In each hotel, resort or complex, each guest will find their own favorite angle, color or texture, and above all, a harmony of the senses. Simply beautiful. You'll see.

usa

hotel healdsburg | healdsburg, ca . usa

DESIGN: Frost Tsuji Architects, David Baker & Associates

No, Healdsburg isn't in the world famous Napa Valley, rather in the neighboring Sonoma County, between the four lesser known (but equally as good) wine regions of Dry Creek Valley, Alexander Valley, Russian River Valley and Chalk Hill. The area is home to over 100 vineyards, complete with all the typical varieties of Californian grapes, and the millions of visitors who come to try them. The other side of this equation are the legendary traffic jams that plague the 101 nearly the whole year round, especially on weekends. And that despite the highway being expanded to six lanes of traffic in each direction in some sections. Those who keep their heads in this chaos are rewarded with a gentle, hilly landscape, a balanced, comfortable climate and finely formed towns.

In the middle of this world-class culinary scenery, Hotel Healdsburg's group of investors have created a modernly designed answer to the rather traditional, sugar-sweet guesthouses and chain motels that proliferate in the district. They have called their project a "prototype for an urban design hotel, in the middle of the wine country".

Their plans were primarily aimed at the young, affluent populations of San Francisco Bay and Silicon Valley, just 70 or so miles south.

Fifty-five spacious, luxurious rooms await the weekenders and business guests who arrive for conferences, spread throughout three linked buildings, situated around a small garden with swimming pool. Hotel Healdsburg's most marked architecural points are the two-story, glass corridor that joins the two largest buildings, and glazed stairway next to the main entrance. The architecture is compact and almost nested, interlaced, but the effect is of neatness and balanced proportions. The unity between external and internal design is also noticeable. There is a strict geometry, a refusal of ornament, and strong coloring that is a characteristic of contemporary, Californian architecture. It is a style heavily influenced by regional factors, and captures the flair of the landscape.

Although the hotel lies in the center of town, right on the corner of Healdsburg Avenue and Matheson Street, thanks to its insulated windows, it is quiet and surrounded by the

01 | The hotel is one of the few
examples of modern hotel
architecture in the heart of the
"Sonoma Valley" wine area.

02 | Buildings, gardens and pool all
have a recognizable, holistic
design concept.

03 04

green of the municipal gardens.
The vast majority of guests are
attracted by this location, with
boutiques, galleries, cafés and
wine-tasting just a few steps
away.

The hotel itself is geared up
towards the high culinary
demands of its guests. Directly
next to the lobby is a room
set aside for wine seminars.
The bar serves the noblest
Merlots, Cabernet Sauvignons,
Chardonnays and Sauvignon
Blancs, often unique to the
region, accompanied by a
choice of delicious cheeses,

but the zenith is reached in
the hotel's "Dry Creek Kitchen".
Head chef and restaurant
owner, Charlie Palmer, already
the subject of critics' praise
in New York, concentrates
on simple, healthy cuisine
created from seasonal local
produce. The "open kitchen"
is a crucial element in the
aethstetic concept of the
restaurant – bright, straight-
lined and transparent.

The guestrooms are also
pure and elegant, a feeling
generated by the warm tones
used throughout, from floor,

writing desk and chairs made
from heavy nutwood, to the
treated, black, quadratic
wooden frame construction of
the TV table. The blinds over
the balcony doors add to the
effect, teasing light through
into the room.

And last, but definitely not
least, the beds must count
among the most comfortable
in America. On a double
matress, wrapped up in Frette
bed-linen, a good night's rest
is virtually guaranteed.

03 | The lobby, with open fireplace, is an open space between the reception, bar, breakfast
   bistro and wine-tasting room.

04 | Corridor alongside the interior courtyard, first floor.

05 | Courtyard with wooden decking. The vines symbolize the hotel's links to its region.

06 | View from the pool through the shading pergola roof, constructed from wicker, towards
   the building which houses the "Dry Creek Kitchen"

05   06

07

08_09

07 | 55 spacious, bright rooms, with sleek, functional furnishings are available to passing tourists, wellness and conference guests.

08 | Directly behind the swimming pool is the small spa area.

09 | Reception. One can gaze down through the glass ceiling from the courtyard on the first floor.

10 | To the right is the entrance area, to the left, the bar is visible through the window.

11 | An example of natural decoration used at the hotel.

10   11

post ranch inn | big sur, ca . usa

DESIGN: Mickey Meunning, Janet Gay Freed

Undulating pastures, vast sandy beaches, pounding waves and white surf. Stark cliff faces, worn smooth by the sea, and mountains over 3,000 feet high.

Long before engineers smashed through the rock to build Highway 1, and put up filigree bridges to smooth its passage across deep ravines, the stretch of coast around Big Sur was already a magnet with special powers of attraction. Well before the first settlers discovered this to be their new paradise, the Esselen and Salinan Indians had bathed in the natural pools fed by the hot springs between the cliffs and the Pacific Ocean. The mystical aura that still surrounds Big Sur today – and which captivated characters as diverse as writers Henry Miller and Jack Kerouac and photographers Ansel Adams and Edward Weston – lies not least in the beneficial effects those hot springs have on body, mind and soul, but also in the interaction with an awesome natural environment. The region was a nucleus for the New Age movement and, with its Esalen Institute, is still a center for holistic medicine and wellness.

When, in 1848, William Brainard Post left his ship in Monterey Bay as an 18-year-old sailor, he certainly would not have had either New Age or the mystical in mind. It was the landscape that fascinated him. He decided to stay, married the daughter of an Indian tribesman from Carmel Valley and created a solidly successful foundation for the Post Ranch. Three generations and numerous local marriages later, it grew to become one of the most important farmsteads in the entire region, and at 1,500 acres, one of the biggest.

Towards the end of the 1980s, William's great-grandson Bill and his wife Luci, together with a few partners and friends, evolved the idea of building a hotel on one of the highest points directly above the Pacific surf. A project that would combine pure aesthetics and natural experience.

Architect Mickey Meunning, an adherent of ecological architecture and organic structures, who had also chosen to make the area his own home, was engaged to draw up plans for the hotel. The 30 guestrooms, restaurant, spa, fitness rooms, library, boutique and reception are relatively spread out over the site and are housed in buildings with very disparate designs, each with a maximum of three "residential units".

01 | The hotel's buildings have been seamlessly integrated into the landscape.

02 | Living and sleeping quarters in one of the Ocean Suites. Behind the terrace is a steep drop to
the Pacific.

03

It is virtually impossible to see the accommodation as you approach the hotel's 98 acres of grounds, and it is not until you reach the car park that you notice the reception, inviting with its spluttering open fire. A narrow path leads from the reception over a bridge to the residential buildings set high up on the mountainside.

There are five different types of accommodation: ocean, coast, tree, butterfly and mountain houses. The stunning ocean houses sit in splendour high above the cliffs, commanding breathtaking views out across the ocean from their floor-to-ceiling windows. From the path, the only recognisable element of the buildings is their roof covering of grass and wild flowers. Inside, the accommodation is extremely spacious. The combination of materials used – wood, glass, stone and concrete – makes for a calming, ordered feel.

General Manager Dan Priano is also particularly fond of the "tree houses", which are built on stilts about four meters above the ground, in among the much taller redwood trees. When swathes of mist from the ocean creep up the mountainside, he remarks that: "You can be lying in bed and feel as if you are swaying weightlessly through the forest – an incredibly inspiring sensation."

The luxuriant natural riches here are a balm to restless souls. Additional help is available in the form of an extensive range of treatments, including myriad combinations of massage, yoga, Shiatsu and Reiki. Also high up on the list of simpler pleasures at the Post Ranch Inn are the wake-up walks in the mornings and the post-lunch stroll through the hotel's herb and flower gardens, fields and meadows.

03 | The boundary between interior and exterior spaces are deliberately blurred, such as here with bathroom and terrace.

04 | Wood is the dominant construction material.

05 | With the fog beneath your feet, spreading out over the ocean, the sensation is of standing among the clouds.

06 | The buildings fan out along the foothills south of Big Sur, overlooking the Pacific.

01 | The roof terrace of the 150,000 square
feet spa complex, containing 36 treatment
rooms.

02 | The Spanish colonial design of the villas
and carefully considered architectural
features meld with the property's long
beaches and gentle hills to create a
balanced aesthetic.

bacara resort & spa | santa barbara, ca . usa

DESIGN: Hill Architects, Glazier Architects, Gary Beggs, Perdian Int. Landscape Architects

At first glance, the site is fantastic. Just 15 minutes north of Santa Barbara, in the center of the Pacific Riviera. With its comfortable climate and stunning coast, comparisons of the region to its French counterpart are not far wide of the mark. At second glance, however, Highway 101 rumbles past, right next door. Then there's the local airport just a hop away, easily as busy as a mid-sized European airport. And then there's oil, albeit below the seabed. A pumping-platform towers above the ocean between the beach and a cluster of nearby islands.

At third glance, these are all just minor deficits. The rushing waves of the sea block out any sound from the trucks on the highway. Even the oil platforms have a certain monumental quality to them, and on the long beach directly in front of the resort is, according to John Hunt, an incredible wealth of native plants, flowers and birdlife. "Sometimes you can see thousands and thousands of butterflies along here", says Hunt, manager of the Bacara Ranch for nearly 20 years.

In 1968, the real estate developer, Alvin Dworman, bought no less than 1000 acres of rough land, from the beach to the foot of the Santa Ynez mountains. The majority of this he turned into a ranch, the heart of which lies in the 40,000 avocado trees that, thanks to their late harvest after the main season, create good profits. "We reach around 75 cents a piece", comments John Hunt. "When the harvest is good, that's real business". But from the beginning , Alvin Dworman had more in mind than avocados. He wanted to create one of the American coast's most exclusive resorts, and from the first design

sketches to the opening at the end of 2000, it took him nearly 20 years. Two decades in which Santa Barbara changed from a sleepy nest with fruit farmers and oil exploration, to one of the most popular vacation areas for the populations of Los Angeles and San Fransisco.

John Hunt shows aerial photos of the earth before the building started. "You get a real feel for the landscape", he says, pointing to the coastline with a pencil. "Seventeen miles of amazing coast to walk or ride along". A few steps next to the resort is the beautiful

03 04   05

Sandpiper Golf Course. On the other side is a new, even more impressive course, due to open shortly. "And everywhere there's nature". Hunt is also convinced that the small oil station, still in the neighborhood, will soon be moved out to the sea. The mixture of oil and tourismis for him untroubling. "That's just the way it is", he shrugs, and leads guests across the ranch, between the avocados, citrus fruits, vegetable farms and herb gardens. A site that the makers have scattered with pathways and picnic places. Alongside a complex that makes itself ideal for events such as team building workshops, the ranch also provides the kitchen and spa with a source of high quality, organic produce. The "Citrus-avocado treatment" for skin is, accordingly, well worth a try.

The spa, overall, is simply gigantic. In a building covering a total of 150,000 square feet are 36 treatment rooms, four complete spa suites, sauna, steam bath, fitness center, swimming pool and the Spa Café which, logically enough, specializes in healthy cuisine. The management of Bacara is also rightfully proud of their gourmet restaurant, Miró. At least three times a week, head chef, Remi Lauvand, and John Hunt discuss the range of ingredients available and those needed for Lauvand's "California Light" creations. "We're always

06

03 | With 368 rooms the resort is ideal for individual
visitors as well as business and social groups.

04 | Landscape designer, Gary Beggs, has harmoniously
linked buildings and environment.

05 | Towel basket in one of the 49 suites.

06 | A view of one of the resorts zero edge swimming
pools. There are three in total; two overlooking
the Pacific Ocean and one more secluded pool in
the spa area.

07 | The blue ceramic tile inlay is an example of
one of the meticulous details found throughout
the resort.

08 09

trying new things out", says Remi. The result is innovative and fresh, complemented by a wine cellar with over 10,000 first-class wines, managed by talented sommeliere, Gillian Balance.

With 311 large guestrooms and 49 suites, extensive conference facilities, spa and gastronomic attractions, the resort is already a small industry in its own right. The buildings, however, are expansive, divided across a 30 acres area, split into smaller complexes. A labyrinth of paths, steps, arcades, galleries and courtyards take the place of long corridors. Each corner offers a new picture. Stylistically, it seems the planners have aimed at a "Mexican village", although the result is sometimes too forced. Despite this, white offers visual consistency, dominating internal and external walls, as well as allowing the garden design by Gary Beggs to come to the fore.

Within a short time, Bacara has achieved an outstanding reputation as a first-class spa and luxury escape for large numbers of affluent and prominent guests, as well as a conference and meeting center. And when all is said and done, that speaks for itself.

10 | 11

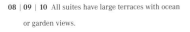

08 | 09 | 10 All suites have large terraces with ocean
or garden views.

11 | In the suites, elegant, adjustable wooden shutters
divide the deep, stone bath tub from
the master bedroom. The stone tub also acts as a
space divider between bedroom and bathroom.
Alternatively, a wooden screen can be pulled
across.

01 | Cactus garden in front of the entrance. The
old name "Cactus Springs" still stands on
the sun-bleached sign in the parking lot.

02 | The former motel's 10 rooms are puristically
furnished and flooded with light.

hope springs | desert hot springs, ca . usa

DESIGN: Steve & Misako Samiof, Mike Haggerty

At White Water, where Freeway 10 leads down into the desert past hundreds of giant, quietly whirring windmills, there is a right turn to Federal Highway 111, which leads to one of America's biggest golfing and retirement paradises. What began in the late 1930s as a handful of lodges and motels in a desert oasis has since developed into a giant that stretches for some 50 miles. Shopping malls, hotels, resorts, golf courses and rest homes for the elderly are strung out from Palm Springs at the western end via Cathedral City, Rancho Mirage, Thousand Palms, Palm Desert, Indian Wells, La Quinta, Indio and Coachella, right up to Thermal in the south-east.

A whole new world opens up, however, if you leave the freeway and head north towards Desert Hot Springs. Wooden shacks with faded "Motel & Spa" signs, a tangle of power cables, barely-used roads and rather neglected palm trees suggest a kind of no man's land. The locals are said to have the quintessential American tendency to "let things be" down to a fine art. The creed of unlimited freedom and individualism also seems to be interpreted here as shunning any kind of joint action.

As elsewhere, it took a few pioneers to rediscover the area's unique appeal and to package it in the right way for the creative world in Los Angeles. Among those pioneers were graphic designers and desert-lovers Mick Haggerty and Steve and Misako Samiof, who, in 1999, seized the opportunity to snap up the very shabby Cactus Spring Motel, which had already been re-renovated to the point of near collapse. Something that would have cost a small fortune in Palm Springs, a mere 15 minutes away, was available here at a knock-down price. They got very excited, laid their hands on half a million dollars and set to work. "Maybe we were just dreaming of lying around our pool with Hollywood stars", says Steve Samiof, when asked what motivated them. Barely a year later, Steve's dream was more or less reality.

The first thing the new owners did was to strip the 1958 property and its ten rooms completely bare. Samiof says, "The decor was a horrific mish-mash of styles. We counted 14 different colors just on the

ceilings, walls and floors". They began the renovation work without any detailed plans although they did have a definite picture in their minds. They summed up their design philosophy, which includes Misako Samiof's purist Japanese influences as "Wabi Sabi", Wabi meaning "beauty through simplicity" and Sabi "beauty through imperfection". "As with any design process, first we created clarity using forms and colors, and then we made a start on the furnishings", remarks Steve.

Most of the walls and ceilings are now in soft shades of

yellow and green; the flooring is cement throughout, sanded and polished. Only in the lobby has the original terrazzo flooring been retained around the fireplace. Another typical feature of the architecture is the separation between the exterior and the interior, with floor-to-ceiling windows and ultra-sleek profiling. At dusk especially, when the indoor lights are on and it is still light outdoors, the aesthetics are quite magical, creating an ideal backdrop for fashion shoots. This was something the owners knew how to exploit commercially, and it brought them and their achievement an

enormous amount of publicity in the creative world.

For the furnishings, antique shops were scoured and bids placed on the Ebay website. There are Saarinen chairs in the lobby, Eames wire chairs on the patios outside the rooms and some well-chosen individual pieces in the public spaces. The three pools have trendy aluminium sun loungers with plump yellow and green cushions. All the pool water comes direct from the hot springs.

In contrast to the rather luxuriant garden with its vivid,

flowery bushes, cacti and rocks, the spacious rooms are extremely purist, with futon-style beds, bright bathrooms, sparsely arranged lighting, simple storage compartments and coathooks. There is neither telephone nor TV, but there is a CD player and a small library with select jazz music. And that's quite enough.

05

03 | A peek into the sleeping area of room No. 4. The
drapes are hung around a meter behind the door.

04 | Transparency is a key theme. At the fireplace, guests
have the feeling of sitting in the middle of nature.

05 | Design classics can be found throughout the hotel's
furnishing.

06 | View across the middle swimming pool to the foyer
and fireplace.

06

miracle manor | desert hot springs, ca . usa

DESIGN: April Greiman, Michael Rotondi

Designer April Greiman and architect Michael Rotondi's original intention was to use the motel built on Miracle Hill in 1948 as a weekend getaway for themselves and their friends. Naturally, word about their idea got around, and their circle of friends soon grew completely out of hand. Although Desert Hot Springs was on the map when Greiman and Rotondi bought the complex in 1997, it was largely ignored by the visiting hordes and weekend commuters from Los Angeles. While one green zone after another took shape in Palm Springs and neighboring resorts, up here the original desert landscape remained intact, along with the constant warm wind and the hot mineral springs. And that meant prices were still affordable.

At the time, neither Greiman nor Rotondi had any idea that they were starting something of a trend by snapping up this bargain. News spread via word-of-mouth until eventually the media picked up on the theme of the insider's tip in the desert.

A discussion of the reinvention and reinterpretation of 1950s buildings followed, which led to a renaissance, which in turn promoted a new style of travel. Purism and reflection on inner values replaced splendour and ostentation as the order of the day. The combination of hot springs and the barren austerity of the desert was suddenly transformed from a natural quirk into an unmissable experience; a location to recharge worn-down spiritual and physical batteries. Bearing in mind Miracle Manor's size – just six rooms – its impact was positively phenomenal, and not least for this reason it attracted other enterprising desert fans to Desert Hot Springs. Two near-by establishments, "Hope Springs" and "Sagewater Spa", provide Miracle Manor with excellent company.

The Manor's two buildings are arranged in a V-shape with the open side around the pool and the enclosed side at the reception which also serves as an office, lounge, kitchen, living room and dining room. While

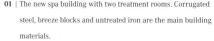

01 | The new spa building with two treatment rooms. Corrugated
steel, breeze blocks and untreated iron are the main building
materials.

02 | Across the swimming pool, a vista of the Coachella Valley
by night.

03 04

rooms one to three are to the "mountain side" of the property and look out onto the green courtyard or the pool, rooms five and six have been built overlooking the valley and have larger windows that afford a better view of the Coachella Valley and the San Jacinto mountains behind.

Externally, the building has almost completely retained its 1948 timber lodge charm. Internally, however, its new owners have really gone to town, eradicating all the accumulated tastelessness in favor of rooms that are calmer, simpler and furnished in a very minimalist style. The interiors are excellent

examples of how to create a relaxed ambience that concentrates on the essentials, even on a limited budget. A prominent feature are the plywood panels used for the floor, for the storage spaces, the desk and the bedheads. The lighting is equally simple, with a dainty halogen lamp by

the bed and a desk light. Walls are smoothly rendered in a hazy grey-green, and the bedsteads contrast in square tubular steel. To complete the experience, have a "Miracle Manor" special massage, crawl into bed between deliciously crisp, cool cotton Coyuchi bed linen and enjoy your own desert dreams.

03 | Sunlight and privacy are provided in equal measure through the use of fabrics in the six rooms.

04 | Plywood is a main material, in the flooring, writing desks and beds.

05 | Reception, public living room and bar.

06 | Entrance area with covered car-port.

01 | View across the completely renovated motel in the San Jacinto Mountains, originally built in 1947.

sagewater spa | desert hot springs, ca . usa

DESIGN: Rhoni Epstein, Cristina Pestana

For anyone for whom the concept of a spa conjures up images of an enormous resort with vast expanses of greenery, complete – wherever possible – with golf course, this is something very different. For a start, the Sagewater Spa with its mere seven guest rooms is so small that it is very easy to miss, tucked away on the small Eliseo Road, familiar to neither the Mexican woman at the petrol station nor the manageress of the local drug store. It is easier and "actually more helpful to ask for Miracle Hill", says Rhoni Epstein, one of the two women who own Sagewater, just up the street from Miracle Manor and Hope Springs.

For Rhoni Epstein and her partner Cristina Pestana from Sao Paulo, "Miracle Hill" is more than just a name. As the two of them stand beside the pool, looking out on the 360° panorama of hills and mountains, they launch into raptures: "Can you feel the energy?" Well…actually yes. You may momentarily wonder whether you have come to the right place, but all newly arrived guests experience a kind of inner calm, shaken with a dash of relief, the moment one of the owners opens the door. As in a select club, you have to ring the bell and explain your presence before entry is granted. With your suitcase stashed away and the sweat wiped from your brow, accept Rhoni's invitation to "Come into the pool!" Once in the deliciously warm water, one can't help adjusting to the new, more relaxed pace of life.

Guests at Sagewater seem somehow to spend their whole time in the pool, probably on account of the wonderful water and its therapeutic effects. At the end of a long journey through the San Andreas Valley, it bubbles up here in the middle of the desert, steaming at 160 °F, pure and enriched with valuable minerals from deep below ground. At Sagewater this constant supply is cooled down to 115 °F before being pumped into the smaller of the warm pools, and 95 °F for the swimming pool itself.

Although they enjoyed a brief heyday in the late 40s and 50s, spa activities were associated in most people's minds with the aged and infirm. Driven by the renaissance of 1950s style, the desert spa experience has since become part of the new chic, and not just in Hollywood.

02

02 | On cool sandstone floors, the high beds are covered with real duck-down quilts and Frette linen.

Successful creatives and numerous personalities have come to Sagewater to cast off their reservations and become part of the temporary, poolside family. Cut off in the middle of the desert, the effect is almost of a very contented mini-society.

When photographers' agent Rhoni Epstein and Cristina Pestara, the former owner of a massage school in Los Angeles, discovered the 1954-built motel, "we knew straight away that we had to have it". What they found was not the least bit inspiring. "Brown fitted carpets, over-ornate furnishings. Everything was very dark, cheap-looking and run-down. What we did like, though, was the location, the incredibly fine water and the architecture of the structural shell". Both women have proved their natural artistic talents. With no architectural training, they went back to what was originally there and optimized it using a simple, sensitive color scheme and choice of materials.

The old carpets were ripped out, revealing a lemon-green stone floor which the new owners sanded and polished. In the kitchen they discovered pink tiles, which were abandoned in favor of more harmonious matching light tones. For the furnishings, their watchword was simplicity. The

03 | 04

03 | Good solutions don't always have to be expensive. Simple soft furnishings covered with colored fabrics fit in to the ambience.

04 | Guests in the seven rooms quickly get down to conversation in the hotel's courtyard; the communications central.

very high beds with their angular steel tubes and multiplex plywood are the work of their friend, craftsman Pierre Kozeley. Together with the modern lights, "old" armchairs and the traditional, fully equipped kitchens, that was the interior taken care of.

Sagewater's structure is arranged in an L-shape around the courtyard and the swimming pool, the main focal point. Each of the seven rooms looks onto the courtyard, with lattice windows that stretch almost floor-to-ceiling and wall-to-wall, generating an ambience reminiscent of an artist's studio, flooded with light. Although the internal space is not large, due to the typical Californian architecture with its seamless transition between the exterior and the interior, the rooms do have a very airy feel. Internal spaces are separated from the courtyard and surrounding desert landscape by glass and screens, and wide white roller blinds for people who really want their privacy.

The air circulates constantly, thanks to the wind that blows here nearly all year round. This does not make the air-conditioning totally superfluous, but means it is only really essential on very hot summer days, when temperatures of around 110 °F are not unknown. But don't come to Desert Hot Springs expecting blazing heat. Here "hot" refers to the water, not to the air. It is always a few degrees cooler here than in the much lower-lying Coachella Valley, home to the famous Palm Springs and neighboring resorts.

There is no separate spa area at Sagewater, as the whole place is a spa in itself. A kind of family villa, so to speak, with an extremely aesthetic ambience, healing waters

and an enormous range of treatments. On request, Brazilian masseuse Livia comes along to your room with all the equipment necessary and a bulging menu of therapies from which to choose. She brings relaxation music too; every room has its own CD player.

Guests mainly arrive at weekends, coming not only from Los Angeles but increasingly from much farther afield. Architects, designers and especially people in the fashion, film and communications industries leave their rather affected business lifestyle behind on Freeway 10 and – after an hour in the pool at most – reappear visibly relaxed, natural and without their corporate sheen. When Rhoni serves her homemade coffee cake (baked to her Russian great-grandmother's recipe), when Cristina mixes her special caipirinha or when an ad hoc barbecue evening is announced, new friendships definitely do spring up. Such a relaxed environment "charged with so much positive energy", says Rhoni, "has already given rise to one or two film scripts". Following one occasion when a writer needed to email his script to Hollywood in a hurry, the two women installed a DSL connection in one of the shady seating areas beside the pool. Now that's service…

05 | The pool forms a central part of life at the hotel, and is more of an outdoor hangout lounge than a place to swim.

06 | Even in summer, air-conditioning is not always necessary, thanks to the cooling breezes that blow over the complex.

07 | A transparent connection between indoors and outdoors is typical for the property's mid-century architecture.

01 | To the left of the corridor is the indoor pool, behind which is the bar and spa restaurant. To the right are the treatment rooms. The Captain's Table can be seen in the background.

enchantment resort & mii amo spa | sedona, az . usa

DESIGN: Gluckman Mayner Architects, Dana Tang, Greg Yang

With its towering red rock-faces, the Coconino National Forest was a magical place for its original Native American inhabitants. In the 1960s, Sedona, located 4,500 feet above sea-level in the center of this remarkable landscape south of Flagstaff, was once again a special place, but for a very different tribe. Its appeal made it into a pilgrimage site for the drop-out generation, and later the New Age movement. In the last 40 years, however, what was once a colony of flimsy dwellings housing "eccentric" individuals has become one of the most popular tourist destinations

in Arizona. For many, the enormous fire-colored stone-formations are a symbol of the Wild West, a real-life cliché and the actual heart of America.

95 miles away, the Grand Canyon National Park steals a certain amount of the limelight, with it's millions of visitors and world-famous name. For the locals, that's hardly a negative thing: "It gives us exclusivity", says the marketing manager of holding company Sedona Resorts, Alexa Hokanson. The region around Sedona is well-visited, although far from being a major tourist spot, with the resort acting as a center of

calm since its opening in 1987. On its 70 acres site, the only sounds are from the wind in the trees, the occasional screech of an eagle or buzzard, and even less frequently, the hum of an Electro-Caddy carrying bath-robed guests from their casitas to the Mii amo Spa, or perhaps from the tennis courts to the restaurant.

Bedded in the imposing contours of Boynton Canyon, the resort appears as a modest village of one- and two-story houses, sitting in a loosely wooded basin. It is an incredible setting, and on arrival, guests are immediately relieved

of their strains and tensions, even before checking-in to one of Enchantment Resort's 220 rooms or the 16 guestrooms and suites at Mii amo . The location alone is the ideal place to recover and relax, but add the Mii amo Spa, and the result is unique. In contrast to the rather rustic casitas, the spa, designed by New York architectural office Gluckman & Mayner, is a text-book example of contemporary architecture that incorporates traditional construction, myths and materials.

The strict geometry of the 150-feet-long main building is

eye-catching. Asserting itself between the natural rock, its materials (loam, wood, glass and stone walling) and powerful color combinations generate a high level of aethstetic attraction. The way to the spa is reached over a natural stone floor, complemented by water features; through an arcade of foliage to the inside of the building and its airy reception. The corridor is a central axis, dividing the building into two parts. On one side are the treatment rooms, and on the other the relax-zones, refreshment bar, indoor swimming pool and access to

the outdoor pool. At its end, the corridor blends into the spa restaurant.

A spiritual highlight is the crystal grotto. A dark, round room with simple wooden benches, natural sand floor, domed roof, and in the center, a large crystal washed over by water. A single hole in the ceiling lets daylight in… but more than just that. The architects, with precise calculation, placed the opening so that at 12 noon, on the day of the summer solstice, 21st June each year, the sun's rays fall directly onto the crystal in

the heart of the construction. In the first minutes of summer 2002, those lucky enough to be present stared hopefully at the stone around which they were gathered. As the first beams struck the crystal, a sensation of fascination spread from person to person, with smiles and contentment visible on the wide-eyed faces. Fascination, and later, a respect for the planners that had created not just a building, but a singular moment, joining together a group of strangers and making them friends.

02 | Indoor and outdoor swimming pools are divided only by room-high glazing.

03 | Wooden, gazebo-style covering at the entrance.

04 | View across the pool to the elongated spa building. The treatment rooms are located in the top floors. To the left is the spa restaurant.

05 | Entrance gate, with the famous red rock of Sedona. The Crystal Grotto can be found in the blue cylinder.

04

05

06 | Top right is the fitness center, behind
the red plaster wall to the left is the library
with internet terminals, as well as the
spa shop.

07 | Entrance area and Crystal Grotto, at the heart of the entire complex.

08 | One of two suites in the Mii amo Spa area. There are also 14 guestrooms here, and 220 in Enchantment Resort.

01 | Fresh air and gold rush atmosphere between the wooden houses and wigwam tents. The saloon is shown here. With 12 accommodations, Dunton Hot Springs has room for just 24 people.

dunton hot springs | dolores, co . usa

DESIGN: George Greenbank, Katrin Henkel and Bernt Kuhlmann

A ghost town. High up in the Rocky Mountains. Not a soul in sight. The wind whips around broken-down log houses; timbers creaking and groaning. The saloon hasn't seen a gold-miner in years, and the barmaids left long ago. A few marmots are the only signs of life, basking in the afternoon sun, their audible squeals mix with the spectral sounds that float strangely around the place. The ruins of the dancehall and the general store rise from the ground like collapsing skeletons, clothed in clouds of steam from the hot springs close by. That is Dunton Hot Springs.

Or rather that was Dunton Hot Springs. In 1994 Christoph Henkel from Germany, and his Austrian friend, real estate manager Bernt Kuhlmann, came across the settlement, 8,000 feet above sea level. "Ghost town for sale" said the advertisement in the local newspaper. The pair came, had a look around, and decided to buy. A complete town, over 800 acres of land, including several hot springs and a 35-feet waterfall. Within seven years, this spot in south-western Colorado once again buzzed with the flair of the gold-rush era, complemented

with the comforts of the 21st century. Dunton Hot Springs is no spartan escape camp for those tired of civilization, however, looking to chop wood and sleep under canvas, but rather a place for visitors treating themselves to the luxury of isolation. Far from tourist masses and package tours, bedded in among the forested mountainsides of the Rockies, the complex today is a lovingly created ensemble of buildings, offering a haven to 24 hand-picked guests. Whether film-makers from Hollywood or wedding parties from Europe, adventurers just

passing through, or managers looking for a modern-day monastic experience.

What was left to restore was built back up by the new "town owners" Henkel and Kuhlmann. Dunton's outdoor chapel, for example, where Bernt Kuhlmann became the first person to marry there following its renovation. The saloon was also given new hope, and now serves as a breakfast room and restaurant; its menu an eclectic mix of regional dishes such as elk meat, served alongside gourmet truffles and champagne.

Evenings, the saloon also becomes a meeting point, with conversation, glasses of bourbon whiskey and a crackling fire. The bulky wooden bar is carved with the names of previous guests from a different age, including the notorious Butch Cassidy and the Sundance Kid, said to have stopped over, having carried out a bank robbery in a neighboring town. The Wild West is alive and well in Dunton Hot Springs. Even in the guest quarters; historical log huts, some of which were cargoed in from other states of the USA, constructed from powerful tree trunks and roofed with corrugated iron that gnashes under the weight of winter snow.

Internally, these houses offer easy comfort. Heated flooring brings coziness, computers with high-speed internet access and video conferencing facilities allow visitors to stay in touch with the outside world. Foreign and ethnic elements are also incorporated into the interior design, and form a definite theme; from the Rajastani bed in the honeymoon suite, the various African masks that adorn walls, to the Native American blankets made of deer leather and the bear skin in the library. A collection of cultures. „After all", says Kuhlmann, "the first settlers here came from all over the world."

In the 105 °F warm springs, guests can bathe under open skies undisturbed, although perhaps watched by Waipiti deer or bears that peer distrustfully from the forests. An alternative is to stay in the "Wellhouse" cottage, where the steaming water flows straight from the mountain into a bathtub, right next to the bed. For more action, Dunton is also the only place in Colorado that offers heli-skiing. Mountain biking, horse-riding, world-class fly-fishing and tours on snow-shoes can also be arranged, to make sure that the soothing effects of the springs are really appreciated after a day in the wilderness. Albeit Dunton's exclusive and eminently agreeable take on wilderness…

02 | Lounge and bedroom with open bathtub in the Wellhouse.

03 | The Honeymoon hut is the largest house.

04 | Light, airy, comfortable and very popular – a wigwam tent.

05 | A unique and pure wellness experience, with open fire and hot springs.

06 | Sleeping area in the "Geyser" property.

amangani | jackson hole, wy . usa
DESIGN: Edward Tuttle

Those who fly into Amangani are greeted with an imposing natural panorama. Left and right, the peaks of the Rocky Mountains stretch out jaggedly, with the snow-capped Grand Teton at the highest point, towering above the valleys below. In the center of these mountains lies the endless space of Jackson Hole, famous for its green fields and dense forests. A winding maze of steams, rivers and torrents run through the landscape, emptying into clear, sparkling lakes. An ideal environment for rare plants and animals, where over 300 exotic species of birds are at home, living happily with the herds of elk and deer, and the solitary black bears.

Amangani, an unusual mix of Sanskrit and Shoshoni languages, means peaceful home. Correspondingly, the building nestles itself into its corner of north-western Wyoming, rising to a modest three stories, and incorporating a range of natural materials. The introverted design blends seamlessly into the mountains, forests and grasslands that form its visual frame. Warm tones of Oklahoma sandstone, Douglas fir, cedar and Pacific redwood create a similar, sincere effect in the property's interior. A gently warmed, outside swimming pool with whirlpool allows guests to wallow and absorb views of the Teton Range, even in the colder months.

Twenty-nine suites, eight deluxe quarters and three top suites are available for guests. All have functional bathrooms

01 | The hall, with its broken stonework, is a good 25 feet high and acts as an enormous
interior stage with an equally as impressive natural backdrop.

02 03

and generous living space, where the iron fireplace can be stoked up, and the rustic, pioneer atmosphere enjoyed, lazing in a cowhide easy-chair. Dark cedar panelling on the ceiling and walls, and various fur and raw wood accessories add to the effect. The impression created throughout the complex is of an exclusive wigwam; in the bar, the lounge, restaurant, training rooms, even in the library. A stay at Amangani is, however, by no means limited to its internal spaces. The number of outdoor activities on offer is staggering, with two national parks within a stone's throw, one of which being the revered Yellowstone National Park. In the warmer summer months, guests are invited to try their hand at fly-fishing, trekking, mountain walking, safari tours, mountain biking or rafting. When the winter arrives, the emphasis switches to skiing, although a less strenuous alternative is to wrap up, and savor a dog-sled ride through the crisp, glistening landscape.

04

02 | Library and reading room.

03 | Pure forms and warm materials in ethnic colors are displayed in
the bar and lounge.

04 | Eight deluxe guest quarters, three top suites and 29 regular
suites are available for the property's affluent guests.

05 | A majestic background for the wonderfully warm swimming pool.

05

01 | The Shore Club was created from the original hotel of the same name, the former Sharalton Hotel and

a new 21-story construction, with a three-floor penthouse. Here is the view from the roof terrace.

the shore club | miami beach, fl . usa

DESIGN: David Chipperfield Architects, Miranda Brooks

Despite a sharp slump in the economy, there is no sign of an end to hotel renovations and new hotel building in Miami Beach. At most, investors and the tourism industry are reporting a slowdown in growth. There is scarcely anywhere else that offers such a range of accommodation in design-conscious hotels than along the endless sandy beach at the south-eastern tip of Florida. Sinking deeper and deeper into mass tourism, Ocean Drive with its open-air art deco museums has been visibly sucked dry. Traffic is at a standstill from late afternoon onwards. Even out of season,

the "cruising mile" – where people come to see and be seen – appears to have lost none of its appeal. And, as you stroll along, you still get menus shoved in your face every few meters by would-be models in bad uniforms. It is almost inevitable that the actual scene people are leaving in increasing numbers for pastures new.

To the south and the north, Collins Avenue, Washington Avenue and Pennsylvania Avenue continue to expand with clubs, restaurants, boutiques and a range of nicely renovated city hotels that grows so quickly it is hard to keep

track. With its pedestrianised area, Lincoln Road, which just a few years ago was still the preserve of locals and long-stay residents, is beginning to rival Ocean Drive. Closer to the beach, tons of concrete have found a new destiny. From the end of Ocean Drive, a voracious urban giant is eating its way northwards, bringing high-rise apartment blocks and hotels, some lavishly renovated, others completely new – or a combination of the two.

One example of this combined approach is the Shore Club, revitalised by Philip Pilevsky. The Bryant Park in New York,

designed by David Chipperfield Architects, is another of his Philips Hotel Group. From Collins Avenue, it is difficult to appreciate the full extent of this resort, offering 325 rooms and 70 suites. Opened in Fall 2001, it is well hidden. The entrance has a rather modest feel and incorporates six floors of the original Shore Club. It is only when you crane your neck that the two residential towers behind come into view. One of them used to be the Sharalton Hotel; the other, with 21 floors and a three-story penthouse suite, is new. Were it not for the pure white and the striking flourish-free facade, you could

easily associate the building with an urban housing project, trying to optimize space. As it is, what hits you in the eye is the minimalist architecture. However delightful the nearby art deco facades with their colorful scrolls might be, by contrast, the simplicity of Shore Club is downright innovative. Instead of stylized flower patterns and endless nooks and crannies, or even fluttery, roccoco-style curtains and motley collections of furniture – disturbingly frequent in Miami –

calm prevails at the Shore Club. Even with the effusive posers you might come across at Nobu's, which has also found a home in Miami.

The courtyards have been given a refined design treatment by landscape architect Miranda Brooks. Long, slim pools of water with shrubs on either side mark out the space between the „towers" and form various terraces, paths and a wellness area with two large swimming pools. The only decorative

features are clay pots with garlic plants arranged in neat rows on flat steps.

In the interior, straight lines and sleek Chipperfield B&B Italia furniture predominate. The floor is a visual treat, with generous stone tiling that continues seamlessly into the bathroom. This is divided into two areas and is separated from the living room/bedroom by a sliding door. Shower and bath are both behind a glass screen, with water from the

wide showerhead flowing straight onto the stone floor. In front are the toilet and washstand with ceramic basin. The frame is teak, as is the rest of the furniture. Everything has been well thought-out and is extremely user-friendly. Okay, so the fixed coir mat before the bed might look a little bit dog-eared, but the sleek forms and pastel tones strike exactly the right atmospheric note for these surroundings, bathed in the glowing Miami sunlight.

05   06

02 | Although the architecture reflects the typical art deco style of Miami
     Beach, the Shore Club is currently the area's most modern and
     minimalist hotel building.

03 | Inside, as well as outside: David Chipperfield's reduced forms.

04 | Shower and bath are both behind a glass wall, although the shower
     falls directly onto the stone floor.

05 | Alongside beauty therapies, the spa complex on the top-floor of the
     middle building offers a wide range of treatments.

06 | Seen from above, the hotel's balanced geometry and colors save it
     from being just another lump of concrete on Miami Beach.

07 08

07 | View from the terrace of the Sundari Spa to the largest of the two swimming pools.

08 | Sofas on the hotel's drive shorten the wait for the chauffeur.

09 | As in traditional grand hotels, the Shore Club has an enormous reception hall. The most adventurous decoration, however, is a wall painting in the background, one or two Zen-style plants and the tea lights, which the staff arrange in different formations each day.

10 | Water is a key theme in the garden design. The landscape architect, Miranda Brooks, has lined the complex with narrow, black troughs. In the bakground are the two-floor Pool Suites.

11 | Arcaded walkways between the reception hall, boutiques, restaurants and spa area.

beach house bal harbour | miami beach, fl . usa

DESIGN: Scott Sanders, Ralph Lauren Design Group

Relax, enjoy the play of light and shade beneath the palm trees and raise your glass to real seahorses – all without needing to stray from the realms of Gucci, Prada and Tiffany & Co. At Beach House Bal Harbour in the north of Miami Beach, you can live out this dream to the full. But once you have sunk into the luxurious wicker armchairs with their fine Polo Ralph Lauren designer cushions, leaving is not going to be easy.

The complex dates from the 1950s and is located on a narrow strip between the smart boutiques of Bal Harbour shopping mall and the Atlantic beach. Following elaborate renovation, the Beach House, one of Jennifer and Jason Rubell's three Miami hotels, was reopened in October 1999. With enormous respect for detail and harmony of style, Scott Sanders, chief designer of the Polo Ralph Lauren Residential Team, designed the resort in the manner of a "luxurious country hotel by the sea".

The hotel's name sets the tone: the ever-present Atlantic is mirrored in many aspects of the Beach House's interior. For instance, the blue of the sea discreetly defines all the 165 rooms and suites – a light shade on the walls and a bold color in the patterns of the gently coordinated upholstery and cushions from the Polo Ralph Lauren collection. Sanders also introduces a Mediterranean counterpoint with white plinth panelling, dark wooden floorboards and light straw-colored wicker furniture with blue upholstery. All suites are decorated with unique finds from the sea – amazing shells or a basket filled with starfish – and each comes with its own mini-library.

If that isn't enough to put one in a holiday mood, then relax in a lounger by the pool or on the hotel beach beneath the ubiquitous palm trees. The luxuries of the hotel's spa will not go amiss either, particularly after the strains of an extended Miami shopping trip. Later, guests can meet up and converse in one of the intimate areas in the lobby. With its wicker furniture, collector's items from the beginning of the 20th century and cosy furnishings, it exudes the charming hospitality of the American East Coast in every detail, combined with the blazing sun and dazzling light of the South.

01 | 02

03

01 | The Beach House in Bal Harbor has more in common
with east-coast flair, than Miami Beach art deco...
a welcome change.

02 | Restaurant entrance.

03 | Although the hotel doesn't look especially large
from the street, it offers 165 rooms and suites, most of
which have a sea-view.

caribbean

parrot cay | providenciales . turks & caicos islands
DESIGN: Keith Hobbs

Is it real? A little corner of the Caribbean without any T-shirt shops? Without a promenade and ice-cream sellers waiting to pounce? Without a single ramshackle wooden hut serving cocktails within view? And no noisy tour groups descending on the buffet like surreal swarms of locusts with pasty limbs and too-short shorts... Just a dream? An island in the turquoise sea which is still undiscovered, still practically untouched, where visitors share the sandy beach with flamingos and turtles. Where the water seems to gleam and a salty tang settles on your lips; where the only sounds are the whispering of the waves and the cries of exotic birds floating across from the island's interior.

Such a place does exist. Parrot Cay is its name, an unpopulated island south-east of the Bahamas which is one of the last unspoilt Caribbean islands. Here, in the group known as the Turks and Caicos Islands, one hour's flying time from Miami, a luxury resort has been created which is the very embodiment of simple elegance. With the atmosphere of an undeveloped natural paradise and the magic of silence, far away from the tourist hordes, complete with all the comforts of an exclusive retreat. The resort, which opened in 1999, has 60 rooms and suites designed by Keith Hobbs from the United Designers team, the man behind the interior of the London Metropolitan Hotel and the Clarence Hotel in Dublin. Whether staying in a Garden View Room, an Ocean Suite or a one-bedroomed beach house, visitors to this island can look forward to accommodation that is elegant and simple.

The main building and villas are built in a modern Colonial style, seasoned with white fabrics that gleam in the Caribbean light. At the center of the rooms stand Indonesian teak four-poster beds, seemingly floating, while a nostalgic ceiling fan keeps the temperature pleasantly fresh, aided by the air conditioning. Every room has a telephone and modem socket, as well as a television and radio, but who comes to a destination like this to watch television?

Parrot Cay is no doubt dream-like, but is by no means solely for guests looking to chill out and relax. There are two tennis courts, a fitness room, and a diving centre invites one to

01 | White is the dominant color. The exterior of the building has a touch of Caribbean flavor, but Keith Hobbs has ruthlessly reduced decoration.

02 03

discover and explore the rich, vivid world of the coral reefs. The resort also offers sailing and windsurfing, canoeing and waterskiing, as well as excursions into the interior of the 400 hectare island, following nature trails through the dense mangroves on foot. Passionate golfers can take a 20 minute boat ride to the main island, Providenciales, with its 18-hole golf course, although everyone can enjoy a little island hopping, soaking up the energy of everyday life on the Turks and Caicos Islands.

For stressed-out visitors, the Shambhala spa center recently introduced by Como Hotels (who also own the Metropolitan in London) provides the perfect retreat. The "center of peace and harmony" is divided into three pavilions which offer a wide range of Asian-inspired treatments and therapies such as the Tui'Na massage, a traditional Chinese method of balancing the Qi energy flows. Or shiatsu, a Japanese form of acupressure which is stress-relieving and deeply relaxing. The Shambhala also

offers beauty baths, such as a seaweed therapy or the "Royal Lulur Bath", a ritual from the royal palaces of Java that begins with an Indonesian massage and culminates in a flower-strewn bath. Dinner in one of the two gourmet restaurants certainly enhances the experience, but in the evening, when the sun disappears in a riot of red and orange, it's a natural show that completes the feeling of regeneration.

04

02 | Bathroom with open-air shower. Wooden flooring throughout creates a natural feel.

03 | The Shambhala Spa has a varied menu of treatments to heal body and mind. Here, one of the relaxation zones with Japanese pool.

04 | Alongside physical treatments, Parrot Cay also caters for a healthy mind.

05 | Modern couches and ethnic furniture is a blend seen throughout the resort.

06 | Bedroom area in a beachside villa. There are 60 rooms, suites, beach-houses and villas.

05   06

water club | san juan . puerto rico

DESIGN: Annie Falgas, Pedro Rosario, Designworks

On the open beach in the island's Isla Verde region stands Puerto Rico's most chic hotel, 11 stories above the palms. With 84 rooms, bathed in blue neon light, the place has positioned itself as a fine, sophisticated city resort, far apart from the huge bed factories that have for so long been part of the scenery here. A short taxi ride from the international airport, the hotel's location is wonderfully quiet. The rooms overlooking the sea are particularly peaceful, as well as comfortably bright, a decent size and with a refreshing design. Due to good transport links to the USA, the

Water Club has developed into a popular Caribbean stopover location. "A stress-free boutique hotel, with a Caribbean beach directly on the front door-step", says Manager, Teresa Keller Rabe.

The hotel opened in November 2001 after a change of owner and a complete renovation. Its architecture shines. Room-high windowed fronts, mostly in the form of bay windows, flood the building with readily available sunlight. Most rooms also offer their inhabitants a fantastic view of palm trees, beach and ocean. Even lying on the bed, the vista is of

endless blue sea and a distant horizon. A fascinating panorama unfolds itself, and is given a fitting frame by the colors and fixtures of the rooms. Storage space is a little short, however – a small niche that combines too few drawers, minibar, safe, ironing board and a clothes rail that's either a kind thought for very small people, or is simply too low.

White walls and blinds that play with the sun, floor panels in imitation, whitewashed oak, as well as the uncomplicated furnishing and black wooden furniture create an attractive environment, whether to relax

in or for creative working. Indeed, it is part of the Water Club's concept to offer an unusual atmosphere for business gatherings, "Nomen est Omen" was clearly in the owner's minds when they named their smallest conference room "Oxygen"; a special place for high-powered meetings that require plenty of the aformentioned stuff in the brains of the participants. The space can accommodate up to 12 people, and invites one to dream with a large bull's-eye window that displays the idyllic beach scene outside. "But the people who are in this room dream together, and that's

01 | Guests are confronted with blue tones throughout the hotel. Design, however, is directed by the sky, sand and sea.

02 | A place for a sundowner on the roof terrace. On one side is the ocean, and on the other is the airport and city.

03 04

05

often when the best ideas and solutions are produced", comments David Kurland. David is one of the two owners and managers of the hotel. Like him, his partner, Joaquin Bolivar, also has a background in the travel industry. Joaquin is the founder of Executive Airlines which today, under the flag of American Eagle, serves the whole of the Caribbean region with a dense network of routes.

With the Water Club, the three businessmen wanted to reach a target group where the borders between work and free-time flow together and overlap. This idea of fluidity has been transferred to the interior design of the property in the form of flowing water, a central theme that runs through the whole building. One can see it behind the counter of the ground-floor Liquid Bar, as a kind of space divider in the entrance area of the hotel, at the end of each story's corridor and even in the property's two elevators. The roof-terrace on the 11th floor is also a remarkable feature; a mixture of scene hangout with sundeck and swimming pool, and open-air lounge (the Wet Bar), kitted out with futons, sofas full of cushions, stripey armchairs, hand-carved coffee tables and an open fire. A romantic spot for a sundowner, when the evening breezes bring a bite to the air, and a spectacular vantage point at night, with the shimmering lights of San Juan on one side and the Atlantic waves on the other.

And all the while, Water Club provides a backdrop of music to complete the experience. By day, the tone is ambient and chilled-out, but as the sun drops, the temperature rises. The main bar kicks off with House and Dance, and the night just starts from there. Before you know it, it's time for your morning massage in the treatment room.

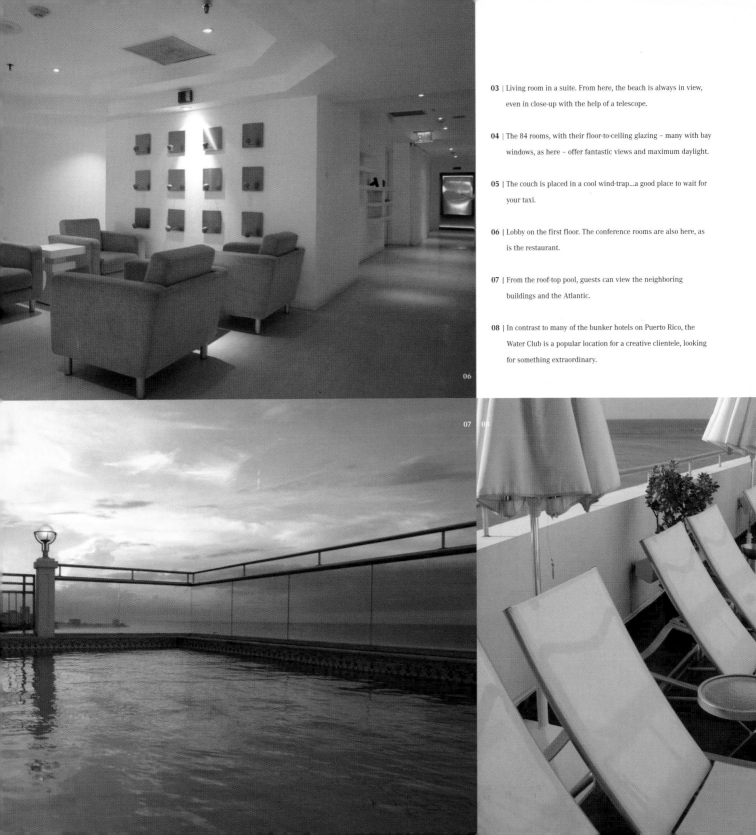

03 | Living room in a suite. From here, the beach is always in view, even in close-up with the help of a telescope.

04 | The 84 rooms, with their floor-to-ceiling glazing – many with bay windows, as here – offer fantastic views and maximum daylight.

05 | The couch is placed in a cool wind-trap...a good place to wait for your taxi.

06 | Lobby on the first floor. The conference rooms are also here, as is the restaurant.

07 | From the roof-top pool, guests can view the neighboring buildings and the Atlantic.

08 | In contrast to many of the bunker hotels on Puerto Rico, the Water Club is a popular location for a creative clientele, looking for something extraordinary.

06

07 | 08

katitche point greathouse | virgin gorda . british virgin islands

DESIGN: Michael Helm

Just to set the record straight: This estate doesn't really belong in this book at all, because it isn't a hotel in the conventional sense. But if you can get a small group of eight to ten friends or relatives together, Katitche Point Greathouse offers all the comfort and service you could imagine in a luxury resort, not to mention a standard of furnishing and a location that are as exclusive as you could hope to find. The unusual thing about this estate is that with weekly rates starting at US$ 9,200 (in the extremely pleasant and highly recommended summer months) for four suites – that

is, for eight people – the cost works out at US$ 1,150 per person. And that includes maid service, breakfast, gardener, pool maintenance and even a laundry service. Even in high season over Christmas, if the house – including the sumptuous master suite – is fully occupied with 13 people, it still only costs US$ 1,372 per person per week. That might still sound expensive for some, but compared to prices of hotels in a similar location and offering similar facilities, it is not only moderate but a veritable insider tip. However, it was not the price and the fact that it is also affordable

for non-millionaires that made us decide to include this Caribbean jewel here. If the word "wellness" is understood to mean a kind of inspirational sense of well-being or, more mundanely, as recharging the batteries then this spot has the perfect mix of ingredients.

First and foremost there's the place itself: Virgin Gorda. It is one of those islands that would make an ideal Trivial Pursuit question, one you'd almost never stumble upon by chance. And it's certainly not among those destinations overrun by mass tourism, even though it boasts a fascinating natural wonder in the form of

the Baths. Giant standing-stone-like boulders are strewn across part of the shore, where they form a jumble of caves, pools, rock climbs and fine white sand bays.

Then there's the location. The estate perches like an eyrie atop a rocky outcrop over the Atlantic, flanked on both sides with idyllic bays that are almost always deserted. From the main house and the veranda there are magnificent panoramic views over the ocean. Here, the vista is not one of endless blue stretching as far as the horizon but a picture painted by nature of countless little

01 | 02

01 | A steel frame supports the three-story main building. From under the pyramid roof, one can see out across the ocean, and under to the library, with DVD, stereo and TV, and dining area on the ground floor.

02 | The complex, comprising four buildings, sits on a rocky plateau between two sandy bays.

03 | Side projection.

04 | Pool and terrace lie around 80 meters above the sea.

05 | Panoramic views come as standard.

islands, slowly circling pelicans and an international boat show. If, on a clear day – and that's practically every day – you were to spend a while gazing into the distance from the boatdeck-like veranda, seated on one of the wooden lounge chairs or swaying gently to and fro in a swinging chair, you would not miss a thing – everything's in sight. It's as if the popular stretch of sailing water known as "Sir Francis Drake Channel" is under your direct control.

The sensitive architecture of the building, including the swimming pool that clings to the rock some 80 meters

above the sea, the array of stone terraces and wooden decks and the original garden landscape, makes the estate a feast for the eyes. Only the most obdurate person could fail to be fascinated. It is a picture that would be hard to match, even in your wildest dreams.

The previous owners had just such a dream when they laid the hurricane-proof concrete slab foundations in the mid-Sixties. But that's as far as the work got for the next 25 years, until another dream was turned into reality here. Working with the American architect Michael Helm, the new owners have

created an intelligent and cosmopolitan paradise on the site. A kind of fusion architecture. Firstly, solid double T supports meet at a 51° angle, just like in the Egyptian pyramids. The roof is covered with wooden tiles. "The steel frame construction has already survived two violent storms", says the architect, convinced that even bigger hurricanes "might tear off a tile or two but won't damage the core structure". Directly beneath the highest point of the roof hangs the so-called "Crows Nest", a steel frame construction furnished with oriental rugs and featuring skylight windows to all four

points of the compass. A Velux door opens out onto the roof, with views over the ocean to the west. This is an energizing, meditative spot.

Down a steep steel ladder is the "Gallery" where guests can watch television – assuming you'd ever feel the need to watch TV here. The room has an impressive collection of films on DVD. But more importantly there is enough room on the couches to make TV viewing a social activity.

The kitchen offers another, more active group experience. Equipped to a professional standard, it reveals a lot about

06 | Bedroom with vista of Mahoe Bay.

07 | Steps to the master suite.

08 | Natural materials and tones in a bathroom.

the passion of the owners for cooking and is enough to make the hearts of amateurs and professional chefs alike beat faster. It is also a visual blast. The very sight of the enormous gas cooker, the refrigerator with its thick glass doors and the ice-making machines makes you want to start cooking straight away – or at least leaves you impatient to sample some culinary delights. But if you don't want to do your own cooking while on vacation you can simply hire your own chef and then sit back and let yourself be enchanted by the resulting Caribbean or international dishes. It seems everything is

possible here: from an elegant wedding breakfast to a rustic barbecue. Depending on how special the occasion, there are a number of different dining venues, just as there are different restaurants in a hotel. Choose between the four meter long solid wood table in the open-plan living and dining area, the kitchen, the bar or any one of the verandas. The possibilities are numerous – certainly enough for a week, at least.

Which just leaves the sleeping arrangements. The master suite is situated at the highest point of the property and, as well as the biggest bedroom,

boasts a free-standing tub. Actually, one edge of the tub abuts a fishpond, giving the impression of a watery front lawn with a roof. To the front and to both sides of the master suite – as everywhere – are verandas with ocean views. The other four rooms are virtually identical in both size and their low-key furnishings. And although they enjoy different locations, in this respect there is nothing to choose between them. Two look out over the palm-fringed beach of Mahoe Bay, while guests in the other two rooms have views of the beaches of Pond Bay and Savannah Bay.

Katitche Point Greathouse is about 15 minutes by car from the jetty where the North Sound Express ferry ties up. The ferry shuttles between here and the international airport on the neighbouring island of Tortola – Beef Island a few times a day, and the crossing takes just 30 minutes. Within easy reach and yet far enough away. The whole island has a population of 2,500 and just two policemen. Locking your doors – that's an alien concept here.

cap juluca | maunday's bay . anguilla

DESIGN: Oscar Farmer, Xanadu - Bob Perkins

If turquoise seas and miles of white sand beaches dotted with palm trees is the stuff of your dreams, you'll find it here in ample quantities. This peaceful island on the northern edge of the Antilles is barely 25 kilometers long and just five kilometers wide. Without the luxuriant rainforests and the steep cliff coastlines found on other Caribbean islands, Anguilla is characterized by a charming, lush green landscape of hills. A total population of around 12,500 means everyone on the island knows everybody else. Were it not for the tropical temperatures and Caribbean temperament, you might think you were in the highlands of Scotland or the foothills of New Zealand's Southern Alps.

Just a quarter of an hour from the small Wallblake Airport, Cap Juluca is at the south-western end of the island, surrounded by lagoons and two bays – Maunday's Bay, the nearest beach where a small peninsula offers protection from any rough seas, and the long swathe of Cove Bay, which has retained more of its original form. The resort's villas are strung like pearls along the white crescent of sand. There are a total of 18 buildings, painted a dazzling white, in a mixture of styles that resists definition, but which betrays Moroccan and Greek architectural influences. Just about every kind of accommodation is available, ranging from a 200 m^2 superior room on the ground floor, to a first-floor luxury room, junior suite or one-bedroom suite, all with panoramic terraces. Or even entire villas with a private pool and three to five bedrooms.

On arrival, guests are greeted by a scene of freshness: white walls, arches, cylindrical and cubic forms compete for attention with palm trees and colorful flowering shrubs. Ceiling fans whirr quietly away in the reception building, where walls with a wash of terracotta shades add a Mediterranean touch. Generally, however, the interior design illustrates a more eclectic approach than the exterior. The shady spaces in the library and media room behind the reception, the decor in hues of brown, and the solid, worn armchairs all remind one of a traditional clubroom scene. The giant TV screen is a slightly brasher modern element, to keep sports fans up to date with the latest football, baseball and basketball matches, but the PC that is also available, complete with printer and free internet access, is a very welcome concession to contemporary life.

Although the overall effect may sound somewhat conservative, there are signs of a more

01 | The powder-white beach is reflected in the building's architecture, in smooth, matt wall surface treatments. Elements from Greece, the Middle East and North Africa are also present in the towers, arches, courtyards and arcades.

02 | A spiral staircase leads up to the roof terrace of a junior suite on the first floor. In the day, these terraces are a little too hot to really enjoy, but by night the views are breathtaking.

01   02

03 04

03 | From outside, Cap Juluca promises a design the interior doesn't
always correspond to directly. Although there may be some breaks in
style, and fabric, color and accessory combinations are not always
completely successful...

04 | ...there are plenty of good examples of fine, functional design, such as
this junior suite.

05 | Louvre doors to the balcony, seen through a mirror.

06 | Bathrooms are bright and reservedly designed, many have two-person
tubs.

07 | Wicker furniture adds to the colonial edge.

05 06   07

ambitious approach to visual balance. Large expanses of white ceramic floor tiles, for example, combined with white walls and chestnut louvred doors, marble bathrooms with generous amounts of glazing, and corner seating areas supported by white stone pedestals in the junior suites.

The new spa area presents another side to Cap Juluca. Already taking shape on the tongue of land between the two bays, it is due to open in the middle of 2003. General manager Eustace "Guish" Guishard sees it as one of the biggest milestones in the history of the resort. Cap Juluca started welcoming guests in 1988 and underwent complete renovation in 2000 following a hurricane. "Juluca is the original name for the local spring where the Native Americans came to purify themselves", says Guish. "A place with spiritual powers". Already, a great deal more is on offer than ordinary massages. The range encompasses holistic preventive medicine, including yoga, transformational therapies and astrological consultations. "All very low-key… we only offer these for guests who are actively interested", Guish emphasizes. "Just as there is a choice between juicy steaks or raw fruit and vegetables, or between pure relaxation and an active vacation with plenty of sport – each to his own".

The manager's sentiments are reflected in the high levels of service that guests experience at Cap Juluca. True to his words, "each to his own", visitors can expect friendly, individual attention. Relaxed, efficient and never flustered, the hotel's team embody the hotel's main qualities, and the reasons why guests come back again and again.

k-club | barbuda . west indies

DESIGN: Gianni Gamondi, Mariuccia Mandelli

The dream of most vacationers is to escape the world for a while, or at least find a part of it that has remained somehow pristine and natural. A romantic idea of living a little like Robinson Crusoe, perhaps, without giving up the agreeable comforts of modern life. Mariuccia Mandelli, founder of the Italian fashion label Krizia, has managed to fulfill this dream in her own corner of the West Indies, on the island of Barbuda. An exclusive resort with a refined ambience, open to a limited number of grateful guests enjoying the life of pampered "Crusoes".

The architecture of the K-Club alone generates a sensation of priviledge. With Gianni Gamondi, Mandelli engaged an architect that had already won major acclaim for his villas on the Costa Esmeralda. The result of his concept is a criss-cross of interweaving buildings, with niches and angles that house seductive courtyards, inviting guests to plan their own rendezvous. Typically Gamondi are the pointed roofs, firing far into the sky, resting on countless pillars. This gives the constructions an almost tent-like quality and provides wonderfully cool, airy rooms.

The inimitably clear colors of the environment inspired Mariucca Mandelli in her interior designs. The turquoise of the ocean, the whites of the sandy beaches and the luminescence of the Caribbean sun are all mirrored in internal spaces. Natural forms can also be seen in the wicker furniture, chairs and deep sofas. Mandelli herself designed the spotted ceramic accessories. All in all, the effect throughout the bungalows is one of noble ease and comfort. Outside showers, hidden among trees, are an undoubted highlight.

Days at K-Club are, however, just as likely to be spent out in the open air as inside the property's elite quarters. Barbuda is home to a plethora of fascinating wild animals and birds, including the Frigate bird. It is almost theraputic to watch its graceful gliding and carefully posed mating dance. Wild boars and pheasants make regular appearances, and are much sought-after as hunting trophies. And the coral reef before the bay opens up a huge range of possibilities for water activities, from gentle snorkelling to wild water-skiing.

With the peacefulness of an ideal sunset, the day is rounded off in the hotel's relaxed restaurant. On the terrace, with a view across the immaculately curved waves, newly baked bread, home-made pasta, fresh fruit and vegetables and delicate seafood make up the taste of an exquisite desert island retreat.

01 | Distant, peaceful and agreeably remote: K-Club lies between
lagoons and sandbanks on Barbuda, the neighboring island
to Antigua.

02 | The resort counts among the most exclusive in the Caribbean,
and is owned by Italian fashionista Mariuccia Mandelli...

03 | ...who also created the airy, white interior.

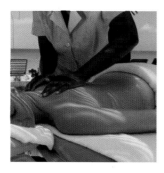

the house | paynes bay, st. james . barbados

DESIGN: Luciano Colombo

A wooden bridge crosses the lily-covered lake. When the hotel limousine carrying newly arrived guests glides across the planks, the surface of the water ripples with gentle tremors and light reflections, mirroring the Caribbean sun, dance between the flowering water lilies. A reserved welcome ceremony. Quietly, almost silently, the island paradise greets its new arrivals. Welcome to Barbados.

"The House" itself is as low-key as this first impression, but this is British understatement in the former crown colony; "The House" is considerably grander than its modest name.

This luxury hotel, opened in 2001, is the latest project of the UK-based Elegant Hotels Group, which has another five exquisite hotels on Barbados alone, ranging from the elegant Colony Club in the north-west of the island to Tamarind Cove, Coconut Creek, Crystal Cove and the Turtle Beach Resort south of the capital of Bridgetown.

Located on the west coast, The House is being heralded by the group as a new standard. A jewel among the palms, a kind of "limited edition" vacation experience in the platinum category. At the island's Grantley Adams Airport,

a limousine waits to pick up another select group of guests. Among them are showbiz celebrities, the international jet set and royals, all looking for one thing above all else: relaxation in an exclusive ambience. The last part of the journey driven by the chauffeur leads down a private road lined by ponds and an evergreen wall of bougainvillaea and tropical climbing plants, whose uppermost leaves glow in shades of red and violet. This is the atmosphere that The House seeks to capture. Open and spacious, sophisticated and free of ostentation. The lobby affords a panoramic view of the Caribbean Sea

stretching away to the horizon. The predominant color is white – the interior, the walls, even the uniforms of the hotel ambassadors. A consciously understated design that trusts in the charm of the surroundings.

The hotel shimmers with shadows during the day, and in the evening is infused with the glow of the sunset. Reverence for the natural environment and its forms – the palms, the tropical blooms – can be seen in the architecture with its use of round arches and wooden pillars, as well as materials that have not been chemically treated. "Eco-friendly" is the watchword at The House

01 | A scene built from stone, wood, canvas sails, palm trees, sand and sea. The terrace of the restaurant Daphne's Barbados, a spin-off from the gourmet temple in Chelsea, London.

02 03

on Paynes Bay, while "Pure Caribbean" is the theme for the hotel's 31 elegant suites. Some have a garden view while others enjoy an ocean vista. Personal ambassador service is available around the clock. Guests can indulge themselves with breakfast in bed, with a special „Flavor to Awaken your Senses" menu, or start the day with a fruit cocktail by the pool and a complimentary jet lag revival massage, shielded by discreet privacy screens to keep out undesired stares. The only sound that breaks the silence is the agreeable background hum of exotic insects and low-voiced conversation.

A wander on the hotel's private beach is a fine way to walk off the first or the last meal of the day. And to keep up one's strength in the sun, a beach service supplies cool drinks and serves ice-cold fruit. "House" guests are also welcome to use the facilities of other Elegant Hotels in the area, including sailing and windsurfing, snorkelling, of course, and canoeing. Alternatively, the nearby "Daphne's" restaurant – an offshoot of the London gourmet temple "Daphne's of Chelsea" – always keeps a few tables reserved for the VIPs from its illustrious neighbor.

02 | Wooden veranda with library, showing the typical colonial architecture.

03 | Bar on the edge of the lobby.

04 | Dark wooden flooring runs throughout the complex.

05 | Lobby: covered, although almost open-air.

06 | With just 31 suites, "The House" is an exclusive retreat, reflected in its prices and clientele.

07 | A sea of vividly colored climbing plants, flowers, trees and palms forms part of the resort.

04

05 06

07

01 | Antique furniture – much from Bali – and European design combine to form a paradisical setting.

laluna | mourne rouge bay . grenada

DESIGN: Bernardo Bertucci, Carmelina Santoro, Gabriella Giuntoli

It has been a steady recovery for this small Caribbean island, from the political chaos that reached its zenith in 1983 with the invasion of US troops. Although in the shadow of their economically stronger neighbors, Barbados and Trinidad, the Grenadines have been spared some of the negative spin-offs that unrestrained growth in tourism can cause. The result for Grenada is an underdeveloped tourism structure, but a correspondingly high preservation of the island's original nature. Its open location between the Atlantic Ocean and Caribbean Sea produces a very mixed climate that, in turn, manifests itself across a wildly varied landscape. While the beaches on the Caribbean Sea coast, in the west, are a collage of gently rolling waves, coral and blond sand; in the east, the angry Atlantic pounds against the land with all its power. Between these two extremes lies a green blanket of hilly tropical forest.

Across the island, one finds hot springs, crater-lakes and blasting jets of sulphurous steam rising from volcanic activity. The highest volcano on the island measures 840 meters above sea level. Compared to such natural might, the only human settlement worth mentioning is the capital city, St.George's; a friendly nest, marked with the influences of its English and French colonial masters, and more recently, by the spending habits of visiting cruise ship passengers. The range of boutiques and craftwork on offer is a reflection of the fact.

Far away from the daily business of St. George's, Laluna is a romantic, bright resort which opened mid-2001. The original idea, however, was very different. After ten successful years in the fashion industry, Bernardo Bertucci was looking for nothing more than a quiet life in his own hidden paradise. After scouring the Caribbean for a suitable spot with his wife Wendy, they finally found their place on Granada: a piece of rainforest, set on a hillside above a sickle-shaped, sandy bay, only accessible over a rocky pathway. "It was much too beautiful to keep to ourselves", says Bertucci. So the couple decided to open up their own Garden of Eden to guests. "We'd never had any kind of involvement in the hotel or gastronomy business before. Then suddenly, the whole thing became a great new challenge for us." Perhaps that's the very

02 03

02 | Open-air lounge as seen from the main steps.

03 | The pavilions housing the 16 guestrooms are built into the
     sloping earth between tropical plants. All have a sea-view...

04 | ...and a wooden terrace.

05 | Terracotta, green and blue tones in wash techniques define
     the interior and exterior walls of the property.

04 05

reason that Laluna has kept its private, personal atmosphere.

The complex, designed by architect Carmelina Santoro and designer Gabriella Giuntoli (who also styled Giorgio Armani's vacation house on Pantelleria), is just 10 minutes from the international airport at Point Salines, but promises idyllic peace, pure nature and an architectural aethstetic of the highest order. With just 16 inviting and functional cottages, the complex has the ambience of a real village, with a blend of styles to match. As Bertucci recalls: "I wanted it to be a mix of various elements – Asian furnishings, ethnic art, Italian food and the spirit of the Caribbean."

The architecture mirrors this in a successful interfusion of Caribbean and Asian influences, led with a European hand and a minimalist touch. Giuntoli and Santoro have artfully interwoven interior and exterior spaces, and although each hut has lockable glass front doors, the borders between in and out are fluid and blurred. From the interior living space, a large wooden terrace stretches out, with plump couches, sunloungers and even a small plunge pool… or an open-air bath-tub with panoramic sea-view, to be exact. Bathrooms and lavatories are roofed, but have only half-walls or blinds to protect one's modesty, and most showers are open to the ocean.

Typical for Laluna is the use of warm, natural materials such as woods, straw and a Mediterranean-style mortar that lends walls and floors a unique, lively touch in cinnamon tones, siena, terracotta, greens and yellows. Strong purple shades, and smooth Venetian-technique plaster surfaces act as contrasts, and symbolize the moonlit night sky. Even when the secluded houses, tucked among the hills, invite guests to enjoy their own privacy and perhaps a butler-served dinner for two on the terrace, conversation and company can still be found.

At the main buildings, on the beach, the open-air lounge has a well-stocked bar, and a small, but fine restaurant, where one can swap stories and experiences with other temporary Laluna villagers.

06 | View of a couch in the lounge, and across the swimmimg pool to the ocean.

07 | In the restaurant, the chef creates dishes of Italian and Caribbean inspiration. The firm, white filets of kingfish are particulary recommended.

08 | The lounge sundeck. In the foreground is the rather small pool, but behind is the golden-brown beach and the Caribbean Sea.

01 | Between broken stone, lush flowers and plants, the hotel offers two restaurants: the Sjalotte with mediterranean cuisine, and the beach restaurant La Plage Hook's Hut.

02 | Easy-going design with quadratic elements and strong color at the reception.

floris suite hotel | willemstad . curaçao

DESIGN: Jan des Bouvrie

„Bon Bini" is the greeting one hears all over Curaçao, in the local Papiamentu language, a mixture of Dutch, Spanish, Portuguese and African dialects that mirrors the origins of its inhabitants.

Just 60 kilometers north of Venezuela, Curaçao is an autonomous Dutch region, linked above all with the color blue: The bright blue of a sweet liqueur that has anchored the island's sonorous name in most European and North American minds. It could also be the illuminated blue of the Caribbean ocean that surrounds the isle, harboring an overwhelmingly vivid underwater world. Whichever way one looks at it, Curaçao shows itself from all angles in a blast of color – even the ubiquitous liqueur is often served in orange or green versions. In Willemstad, the capital, it doesn't take long, with the help of a cocktail or two, before the Dutch colonial architecture begins to instill the local state-of-mind, full of light-hearted curlicues and powerful Caribbean tones.

On a stroll through the city, your eyes fall on fine jewelry, valuable antiques and designer fashions, all displayed in exquisite boutiques to Curaçao's guests, and those of the luxury liners docked in the port. In dignified pace, the old trading center opens its historical pontoon bridge to the floating palaces which sail into the harbor, towering as shadowy skyscrapers over the swirling, Hansel-and-Gretel-house skyline of St. Anna Bay.

Ten minutes by car from the historical center of Willemstad is the Floris Suite Hotel. Opened in August 2001, it is an example of first-class, simple luxury, with the architecture of the property successfully combining European colonial style with Caribbean elements, blending agreeably into the surrounding scenery. Jan des Bouvrie's design is clear to see in the modern translation of colonial comfort displayed throughout the 72 suites, and their clear-lined exotic touch. In these rooms, cool natural stone floors correspond with warm mahogany, and sumptuous but elegant furniture fits with the noble materials of the accessories and fittings. Leaving their private patio, part of each of the 32 Royal and 40 Junior Suites, guests can find company in the Floris Suite Hotel's lush tropical garden. Here, shady terraces and an open-air restaurant invite one to stay for a while, perhaps to contemplate a dip in the large swimming pool, located in the middle of the garden landscape.

The only competitor to the hotel's seductive atmosphere is its petal-white beach, one of the island's most beautiful, with a bar and restaurant offering all the cocktails and seafood that one could wish for in a Caribbean idyll, along with the glassy sea, full of parrot-fish. A little less romantically, visitors driving across the island with a hire-car will come across

the gigantic refinery at the end of the capital city, at the oil port. Not only is 90 percent of Curaçao's gross domestic product produced here, but also a range of unpleasant odors that can occasionally change the nature of the otherwise welcome sea-breezes.

Nonetheless, a drive across the spartan, hilly landscape is an adventure, and a chance to see the well preserved plantation houses that serve

as evidence of Curaçao's agricultural past. Today, the contours of the earth are filled with cactus and spiky thickets, home to goats and lizards, rather than the cotton, corn and fruit plantations that were once the economic lifeblood of the island. The best beaches lie hidden in the south, reached along winding narrow tracks. The northern coast is, in comparison, unapproachable. Its stony outline is just as raw as the raging sea that crashes

against it, gouging out deep caves in the cliffs. Rising above this vista is the Christoffel Mountain, at 372 meters above sea level, the highest mountain on Curaçao. From its peak, it offers endless views, encircled by tropical forest at its base. Here, in the national park, where humming birds zip between multi-colored flowers, one really feels close to South America… say about 60 kilometers away.

03 | Lamps in an open-air walkway..

04 | A junior suite terrace.

05 | Statue in the lobby.

06 | Bedroom in one of the 32 Royal Suites.

07 | From outside, the complex also presents itself as an example of modern colonial style.

08 | Bar, restaurant and lobby are partly indoor, partly roofed, and partly open-air.

mexico

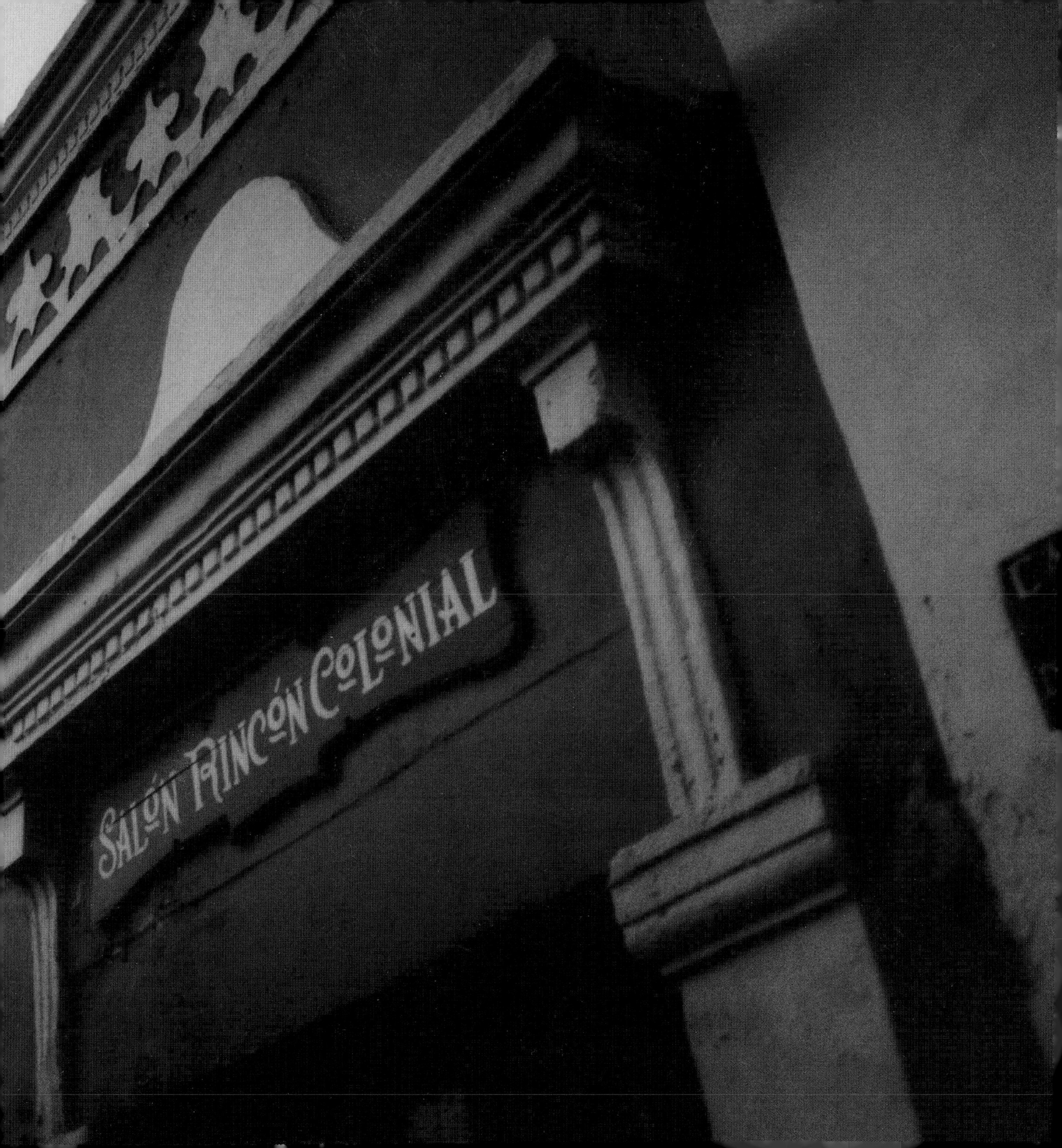
SALÓN RINCÓN COLONIAL

verana | puerto vallarta . mexico

DESIGN: Heinz Legler, Veronique Lièvre

It's the search for untouched places on earth that repeatedly brings new travel destinations to light. And it takes people motivated by the need to find and create something special, to carry out the search. Heinz Legler and Veronique Lievre definitely fit into this category.

After an adventurous journey, Heinz and Veronique arrived by boat in this isolated bay on the west coast of Mexico. A mule helped them up the last meters to the top of nearby mountains, where their effort was rewarded with views of an untouched paradise. A lush gate to the jungle, framing distant coastal hills and the Pacific Ocean. A place full of primitivity and inspirational power that the couple transformed into an exclusive, intimate resort, even though their original plan was to build a home for their own retirement. Since November 2000 guests can also share Heinz and Veronique's comfortable isolation and closeness to nature, in one of the six individually designed bungalows available.

Each of these accomodations has its own name. The most natively styled of these is called "Palapa", and appears as if built on ancient ruins, largely without any kind of separating walls. Over the stone niches and diverse levels rises a high roof constructed from tree trunks, simply covered with vegetation from the jungle. The "Studio" shows, in comparison, an elegant but harsh design. Together with its wide windowed front, this dwelling offers a markedly artistic atmosphere. "Stone House", „Mayan", "Casa Grande" and "Bungalow" all successfully blend the trappings of modern living with traditional crafts and forms. The strong natural colors of the Tropics dominate the choice of accessories and fabrics in the rooms.

Overall, it is the organic interplay of internal and external concepts, of rustic and modern, of natural

01 | The property is only accessible by boat, and
the last few meters by foot. The journey is
rewarded with panoramas such as this.

02

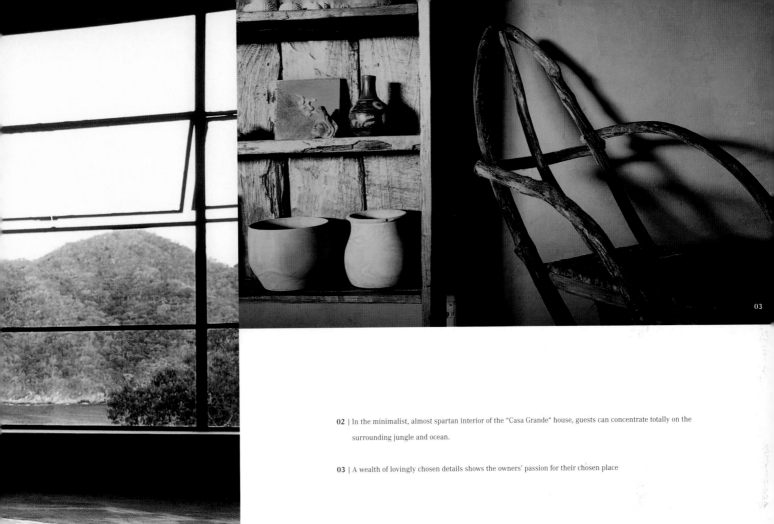

02 | In the minimalist, almost spartan interior of the "Casa Grande" house, guests can concentrate totally on the surrounding jungle and ocean.

03 | A wealth of lovingly chosen details shows the owners' passion for their chosen place

and man-made, and of openness and privacy that gives Verana its particular charm. A charm which makes itself felt throughout the property, whether in the colorful, Mexican-style kitchen where the chefs produce their wonderful crossover creations, when chilling out on a terrace, looking through the library's books or taking a dip in the cool mountain water of the pool. Or in the evening when, looking into an endless, black starry sky, oil-lamps and candles flicker.

The silence of civilization is all around, but the night belongs to the jungle…

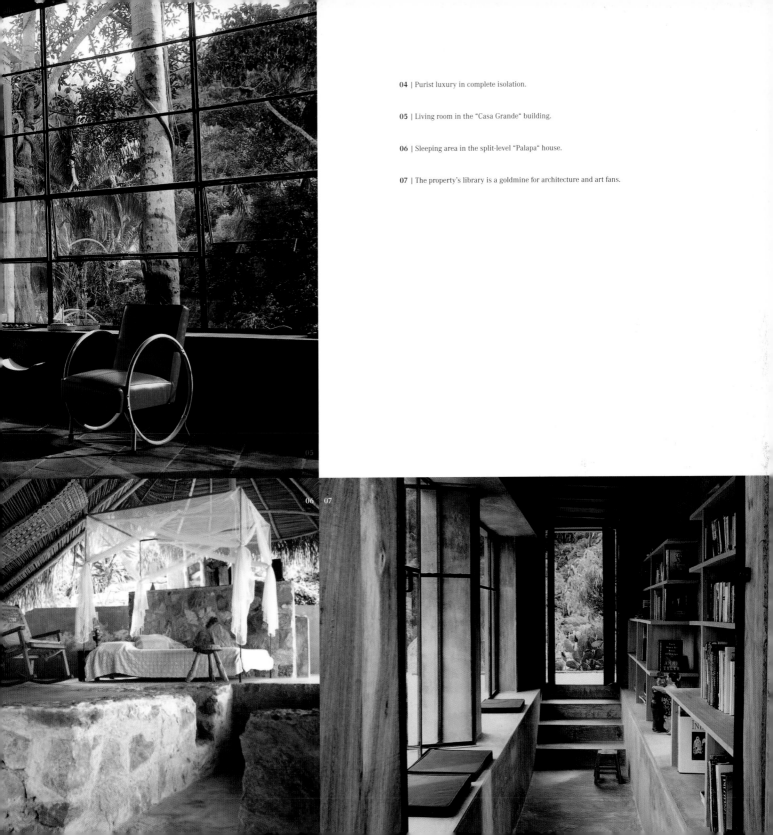

04 | Purist luxury in complete isolation.

05 | Living room in the "Casa Grande" building.

06 | Sleeping area in the split-level "Palapa" house.

07 | The property's library is a goldmine for architecture and art fans.

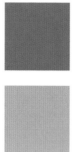

hotelito desconocido | puerto vallarta . mexico

DESIGN: Marcello Murzilli

To the south of Puerto Vallarta, Highway 200 becomes an almost car-free zone, as this section of the Pan-American Highway meanders through the thickly wooded area along the coast. Anyone making the journey for the first time by car would be well advised to do so during the day. Roadsigns are few and far between, and those that do exist are not particularly clear, even when the sun is blazing down. Some 90 kilometers – or around an hour and a half – to the south

of the international airport, a sign points down a gravel track towards Cruz de Loreto. Another 18 kilometers and you reach Cruz de Loreto, a village in a shimmer of heat on the edge of nowhere. Now you need to rely on your instincts and keep to the right-hand side of the pothole-covered clay roads. Sooner or later, a sign mentions Hotelito Desconocido. Drive through a small oasis and, around two hours after leaving the airport, a driver with an average sense

of direction should have reached his or her destination.

It's worth it: a coastline of sandy beach stretching as far as the eye can see and interspersed with lagoons, marshes and pastures, well away from anything remotely resembling a tourist settlement. The idea of establishing a luxury resort – the only one of its kind to date – in this isolated corner of heaven was the brainchild of Italian fashion designer Marcello Murzilli. In the early

1970s, Murzilli founded the "Charro" label. By 1991, he had had enough and sold the business, by then a fully-fledged empire. During his business career, this versatile Italian was part of the Formula 1 scene, with a team of his own, and even won the Paris-Dakar Rally with his Honda-Charro team. Following the sale of his company, Murzilli swapped motor engines for sails. He sailed round the world, and it was on the high seas that he came up with the idea of

01 | Not a shadow-theater, but an open-air
massage under breeze-wafted mosquito nets.

02 | With just 29 palafitos (living huts) and
40 hectares of grounds, the Hotelito has a
private, but familiar atmosphere.

03 | 04

combining nature with luxury, and of linking ecology with design by creating a hotel.

As is so often the case, 'hotel' is not really the right word in this context; 'hotelito' has a much warmer ring to it. In fact, the 'hotelito' is the incarnation of a romantic fishing village with simple villas. The aesthetics are crucial: in virtuoso fashion, the designer of this dream complex has pulled off something which, almost invariably, seems somewhat forced in a club

village scenario, however good the intentions. Subtly nuanced shades and painting styles are juxtaposed to magnificent effect with strong colors and techniques. The planning, the fine detailing and the decorations all reveal Murzilli's assured feel for visual balance. Strolling around the site is like leafing through a new hybrid between design journal and travel magazine. Apart from the natural surroundings, which provide an ever-changing backdrop, nothing has been left

to chance. Neat paths, well-chosen antiques from all over Mexico, the bar – vibrant with color and brimming with table lanterns – the restaurant with its lagoon-side deck, the spa facilities, the observation tower, the beach pavilion and the villas themselves all show the couturier's signature running through everything like a thread. The staff wear loose white linen suits, with colorful headscarves.

With just 29 accommodation units dotted around two of the

total 40 hectares of grounds, there is a certain amount of privacy, although the walls of woven bast are thin, the strung skylight flaps are light, and the doors to the terrace let the air through, which is just as well. There is a virtually unobstructed view of the outdoors from the shower/WC, and vice versa, which means the animal kingdom is always in view, and there is a great deal to see here. Hundreds of different species of birds, crawling creatures of all kinds

05 | 06

and even the occasional
armadillo tootle around among
the dwellings, which are built
on stilts. True luxury, however,
lies in there being no telephones,
and certainly no TV; even electric
light is banned in favour of
candelabra and candles. Only
the fan above the mosquito net
is powered by electricity – and
a good thing too. Although
temperatures do cool down very
slightly in the evening, almost
all guests confirm that anyone
who survives the first night in
these unfamiliar surroundings

03 | Relaxation in the open-air spa area.

04 | Each of the guest quarters is individually designed
and decorated.

05 | Even the beds are different: sometimes made from wicker,
some are wooden and some are forged from iron.

06 | A central point of the complex is the observation tower,
next to the bar and restaurant. Guests can take a boat to the
beach on the opposite side of the lagoon.

07 08

and manages to get a decent night's sleep will sleep like a log for the rest of their stay. In an environment like this, keys are just as superfluous as laptops, and room service functions as if you were lounging in a luxurious beach chair. To order coffee when you wake up in the morning, you raise a little red flag on a pole above the roof. Minutes later, an attendant arrives carrying a tray of fresh cookies and some "Mexican special blend" that tastes strongly of cinnamon.

If you fancy the beach or the swimming pool, there is a spot of work to be done first, because they are across the water. A small armada of brightly painted rowing boats awaits to ferry you across. If you haven't the nerve to row, or are simply feeling too lazy, a rowing attendant is on hand to assist. The time you are likely to appreciate him most is after an enjoyable dinner accompanied by Corona beer, tequila or wine, when you are heading off in one direction or

another – though probably not to your bed in one of the 12 beach "palafitos".

Hotelito is not just the ideal hideaway for romantics but is also a vivid natural experience and a reminder that simple is beautiful. A new definition of luxury, or, as Marcello Murzilli predicts in his brochure, the hotel of the third millennium. Seems like a reasonable statement to make.

07 | Reception with library.

08 | A Lagoon Suite terrace. From here, one can gaze across at the waves on the beach opposite.

09 | 10 Marcello Murzilli has created his nature-hotel with a sensitive feel for color and detail. The only electricity in the guest quarters powers the fans; light is provided by candles and lamps.

11 | Each hut has its own name. Here, the view from "Tamburin" across the terrace and lagoon, towards the hinterland.

09

10 11

01 | This pool villa, in the vacation complex „Casitas de las Flores", lies above a fine, sandy bay.

02 | The powerful colors are an essential element of the complex's Mexican architectural style.

casas de careyes & casitas de las flores | costalegre . mexico

DESIGN: Gian Franco Brignone, Marco Aldaco, Diego Villaseñor, Jean Claude Galibert

As Europe's students were taking to the streets crying, unsuccessfully, for world revolution, Gian Franco Brignone was setting off for Mexico. He was long past student age and light years away from street activism. Already 40 and with a familyof his own, Brignone was upholding the respectable family tradition as a banker in Paris, until in 1968, of all years, he changed his mind. He had fallen for a romantic, wild stretch of Mexico's Pacific coastline. Despite a gamut of fine sand beaches, steep cliffs, rocky islands jutting out of the ocean and idyllic, isolated bays, few people were interested in the place, in those days. With a

head full of ideas and a wallet full of money, he flew to Mexico to start a new life. A life as a visionary with a passionate belief in a better and, above all, more beautiful world. His dream was to exalt and enrich nature through his own inspirational ideas and fantasies.

Brignone's creative achievements over more than 30 years are dazzling: 42 villas scattered far and wide, aesthetically stunning, masterly in construction and design and all with a magnetic aura – they alone could fill a whole book on architecture. The perfect symbiosis of colors, forms and materials and a sensitive integration with

the environment point to an intellectual and creative proximity to the work of Luis Barragan.

The designers do not make any secret of their great respect for that exceptional Mexican architect. Fundamentally though, architecture can only ever be as good as the client will allow. In Gian Franco Brignone, the architects and designers Marco Aldaco, Diego Villaseñor and Jean Claude Galibert found an ideal counterpart. A powerful, dynamic eccentric who made vision and passion his top priority long ago. Any "sensible" businessman would have dismissed their ideas as madness, but former banker

Brignone had a shrewd understanding of the finances involved. In his own lifetime, he managed to construct a memorial to himself – his output includes dream houses built in several stages, other individual properties for sale or rental, the Casitas de las Flores community, and the El Careyes hotel complex, which has now been sold to Grupo Plan and is operated by Starwood.

Nevertheless, business cannot really be said to be booming, and although only an hour and fifteen minutes drive from Manzanillo Airport, and two and a half from Puerto Vallarta, the coastal location, known

03 04   05

as the Costalegre, is still
pretty secluded. Despite that,
Brignone's son Giorgio, who
manages the property and the
associated business, and
generally keeps an eye on
things, has certainly inherited
his father's passion.

The creative family spirit
pervades everything down to
the last detail. One senses that
the Brignone family themselves
would be happy to live in any
of the properties. Sol del Oriente
and Sol del Occidente are the

two „flagships". Two buildings
opposite one another, perched
in splendour some 50 meters
above the sea and separated
only by a bay Brignone has
christened „Angels' Bay".
These are the cumulation of
his legacy and symbolize the
fusion of his cultural influences;
his own personal way of
expressing peace. Underneath
the palm roofs, visitors are
greeted by a modern fairyland.
Mirror ornaments and a mixture
of colored stones and painting
techniques blend together to

create artistic images. The purist
decor is equally spellbinding:
a great deal of stone, several
museum-style antiques and the
hallmark generous day beds
everywhere, piled high with
cushions. There are few proper
doors or windows; the walls
have openings instead, some
wide and some narrow, acting
as picture frames, they
encompass the innumerable
vistas where architecture and
nature meet. Like a moat,
turquoise swimming pools run
almost a full 360° around these

jagged, circular edifices. Guests
can swim towards the sunrise
in the morning and watch
the sunset from the water in
the evening. An unusual,
more energetic and eminently
exclusive leisure pursuit that
the property also offers is polo,
giving guests the chance to
try their hand or polish up their
skills at the "sport of kings".

Mi Ojo, another total work of
art, sits majestically several
clifftops away. Again vibrant
with color, it has a breathtaking

03 | Open planning, and a seamless transition between bedroom, kitchen, living quarters and terrace. A suite in the Casitas de las Flores.

04 | Bedroom over the cliffs. The open terrace doors lead straight onto the rocks.

05 | A view through one of the wall openings in the Sol de Oriente.

06 | Mosaic in the entrance hall of the Sol de Oriente.

07 | Like a moat, the swimming pool is built around the central building, a good 50 meters above the sea.

06

07

hanging bridge between the cliffs. There are eight bedrooms, a variety of semi-open and fully open living spaces and a professional kitchen – a total living space of around 1,000 m² offering pure luxury for up to 16 people. It comes complete with a cook, maids, gardeners, a poolman and even a chauffeur, if required. But the agonizing choice is far from over. There are also the villas at the intimate Playa Rosa: Casa las Conchas with three bedrooms, and Casa la Huerta, Casa Altiplano and Casa los Candelabros, each with five.

There are places that are more affordable too: Casitas de las Flores village, for instance, modelled on a picturesque fishing village, has apartments with between one and four rooms. In a fantastic location with views of the sea, spacious airy rooms and a masterfully orchestrated blend of folklore, minimalism and functionalism, they could become a regular retreat for those who have made the journey to reach them.

08 | From one of the numerous roof terraces of the Mi Ojo, on the northern edge of the complex, the panorama is one of ever-changing coastal landscapes. The breathtaking rope-bridge leads to an unihabited private island, that counts as part of the villa.

09 | Local artistic themes run throughout the Brignone's villas.

10 | A cosy, shady corner at Villa Mi Ojo.

11 | Although strong colors dominate the exteriors, white is the prevalent interior shade, often with glossy effects.

12 | Circular swimming pool at the Sol de Oriente.

01 | Originally there were 11 different colors, then
just white. Now, since 2001, the colors have
returned to El Careyes again, such as here in one
of the numerous walkways. The turtle, as mosaic
inlay, is the hotel's mascot.

02 | Between the hotel and apartment buildings,
guests find boutique-filled passages.

01 02

el careyes | costalegre . mexico

DESIGN: Diego Villaseñor

Lush tropical forest and a thrilling mix of almost inaccessible rocky cliffs and tucked-away sandy coves. Always warm but rarely humid, thanks to the fresh sea breezes. In short, the perfect place for a leisure resort. That's what Gian Franco Brignone and his son Giorgio thought at the end of the 1960s when they created this unusual holiday hacienda, comprising a 40-room hotel and an apartment building, amidst the coconut palms between two hills on one of the coast's shortest and most well-hidden sandy bays.

The complex sits perfectly in the narrow inlet, as if it were part of the natural landscape. The buildings are grouped in a horseshoe around the beachside garden and pool complex – a swimming pool with so many curves and bends that it looks as if the designer simply dropped a large load from a firefighting plane to create a water labyrinth with islands, bridges, shallows and depths, sunny and shady spots. Straight lines are few and far between. The horizontal and vertical accents on the interlocking buildings, on the other hand, could have been drawn with a ruler. External walls, balconies, patios and rows of windows create an effect that is classical, even verging on the unspectacular. But that's certainly not to say dull. The necessary contrast is created by the arches that shape the passages, walkways and windows. And the way in which the complex as a whole has been arranged, with a wealth of interesting angles, means there is a visual surprise around every corner. Steps lead from the outside into the interior and back outside again, around corners and through loggias.

The complex was taken over by Grupo Plan in 1992 and is now run by a management company under the Starwood Luxury Collection name. The new owners have replaced the delicate pastels and white-painted walls with stronger colors and have picked out edges, recesses and the occasional section of wall in complementary tones. "The salty sea air means that white doesn't stay white for long – and more intensive colors are more Mexican anyway", remarks Rui Reis laconically. Originally from Portugal, Mr. Reis has been a director here and at the sister resort of „El Tamarindo" since June 2001. He particularly likes "this riot of colour" at El Careyes. "It's just very cheerful".

03 | 04

In fact the playful aesthetic has an air of "feel-good" about it. True, not all the guests bound along the corridors and across the terraces and beach with big grins on their faces but a feeling of deep, inner tranquillity is instantly noticeable. Particularly after a dinner of freshly caught fish, such as grilled fillet of dorade marinated in coconut milk, with steamed vegetables and rice.

The restaurant tables are scattered around the covered bar and across the tiered terraces with views over the sea, the bay's two promontories and the islets and rocks in between. Whether eating breakfast, lunch or dinner under the light of the moon, in this setting even french fries and ketchup could become a gourmet experience.

The resort's celebrated "cuisine of the water gods" is based on recipes of Patricia Quintana, a well-known writer of cookbooks, who has created light and delicious menu suggestions from a tour along the Mexican coast, which fits in perfectly with the spa concept. Alongside the usual types of massage, the focus here is on preventative medicine or put more simply, health-conscious living. The approach is holistic, from the right diet to exercise and relaxation techniques with yoga, massages and aromatherapy, through to complete therapeutic programmes.

The perfect day starts with a refreshing early-morning dip in the ocean, followed by yoga or tai-chi on the beach. The well-deserved cup of green tea tastes best on one of the cushion-scattered couches in the palapa pavilions. An aesthetic delight and the best possible place to lounge about – all you need now is the right music. Stretch out and enjoy. That's relaxation. The Brignones were right.

03 | A view from one of the five ocean front junior suites. The plunge pool is directly linked to the bathroom.

04 | Every story and arcade is differently designed.

05 | The white louvre doors and blinds create a comfortable temperature, and an absorbing light and shadow effect. Here, one of the junior suites, with sea-view.

06 | Red and blue are the dominant colors, on walls, pillars and door frames.

el tamarindo | cihuatlán, jalisco . mexico

DESIGN: Luis Bosoms, Grupo Plan

The cloudburst lashes at the windows of the twin-engined ATR42. Despite it being a full 20 minutes since the small plane began its descent, there is still no land in sight, just the slightly unnerving view of what appear to be approaching waves. Wild streaks of lightning jerk towards the water, and it seems as if the pilot is earnestly attempting to land his craft on a foaming sea. Just before the ocean swallows us up, the undercarriage opens and there is asphalt beneath the tyres. The rare Storms on Mexico's west coast are quite peculiar.

Negotiating the route from Manzanillo Airport to El Tamarindo by car in this kind of weather promises to be a serious adventure, especially in the dark. There are not that many opportunities for losing your way, but when that one crucial road sign is obscured, you'll find yourself driving into what seems like endless pampa. If you do have to take the wheel yourself, try to do it in broad daylight, and stick to Highway 200 along the coast towards Puerto Vallarta. After 50 kilometers or so, take a left turn onto El Tamarindo's

immaculate driveway, with its neat mosaic of cobblestones. The best way to appreciate the scale of this vast, 850-hectare paradise with its more than 15 kilometers of coastline and three private beaches, is to take a tour in one of the electric cars on site. The centerpiece is the 18-hole golf course designed by Robert Trent Jones, Jr. and David Fleming. It is no exaggeration to say that this is one of the most spectacular golf courses in the world, taking golfers through tropical forests, across hilly parkland, past sheer

cliffs and sandy bays. A visual cornucopia accompanied by the sound of birdsong, frogs and crickets. An unusual seasonal sight are the thousands of crabs that scuttle around thearea, risking being crushed underfoot each time a guest goes for a stroll, or even worse should someone take one of the electric carts for a spin.

The natural spectrum on show at El Tamarindo is breathtaking. There is only one thing missing: people – or at least that's the perception. The thoughtful distribution of a mere 29 villas

02

01 | Guests at the property are always exposed to nature. Half of this beach villa can be opened to the fresh air, with sliding doors and walls.

02 | The grounds of El Tamarindo stretch over no less than 850 hectares. This private hotel beach, with romantic massage hut, is just one of many.

03 04

05

over a large area yields a great deal of privacy and gives the impression of an absence of people, even when the entire resort is occupied to full capacity. Peace and quiet, exclusivity and deserted bays remain the order of the day.

For people looking for an intimate retreat, the Palm Tree Villas, some of which have two bedrooms, the Garden Villas or the Forest Villas offer the

greatest degree of seclusion. The best option for those seeking a little more social interaction is a Beachfront Villa. These offer the shortest route to the golden-yellow sand across a closely mown lawn. All accommodation is in "palapa style" – bungalows with pointed roofs covered in palm fronds. The furnishings are simple – almost too sparse. Anyone thinking of doing a spot of work, for example, or enjoying a meal

indoors, will be disappointed – the only proper tables are outside – but that reflects the fact that life here is lived more outdoors than indoors. To facilitate moving seamlessly between the two spaces, there are double sliding partitions. One pair is made of glass, the other has slats and a fly screen. Having them open creates a covered living, sleeping and relaxing area with its own terrace, garden and plunge pool.

The combinations of materials used reflect the natural theme: clay, wood, glass, straw and a cool floor with decorative pebble ornamentation. Colors and forms blend harmoniously. It is an unadulterated pleasure to escape to one of the day beds with an armada of small, plump cushions and let your gaze wander.

Although beautifully situated between the beach, the buildings

06

03 | Honey-yellow and ochre tones make up the
facades, and floors are decorated with
millions of pebbles. Even the approach road
to the hotel, around 7km long, is covered
with this mini-cobble stone effect.

04 | The sliding walls can also be shut tight. In
the foreground, an inviting daybed.

05 | Private approach to one of the forest villas,
hidden between tropical trees, palms and
huge ferns.

06 | Even the most jaded of golfers are astounded
by the beauty of this 18-hole course. Most
of the guests, however, don't even know
what golf is, and are more concerned about
finding a mate...the greens are seasonally
invaded by thousands of crabs from the
nearby beach!

and the lawns, surrounded by
a swathe of chestnut-brown
wooden decking, the main
swimming pool is hardly a place
to swim. It may be adequate
for a few strokes but sporting
types will reach the other side
rather more quickly than they
would like. It is surely meant as
a place to take a quick dip, or
for guests to recline in the mere
five centimeters of water at
the pool's edge, armed with a
cocktail from the nearby bar.

The spa offers a more authentic
experience. It has an adjacent
"jungle gym" and a Mayan
steam room, or temascal, an
experience that guarantees
physical purification deep into
the skin. This is a pre-Hispanic
ritual where standard therapeutic
mud rubs are combined with
purifying saltwater treatments,
accompanied by an opening
up of the spirit in sweltering
heat, in darkness and to the
sound of drums.

07 | Gallery in the reception.

08 | A spot to linger.

09 | Even the way to the restrooms is with hand-made one-offs and
     tasteful accessories.

10 | The pool deck, just before sunset.

11 | The property's spa offers a huge range of beauty and health treat-
ments, as well as an authentic local experience in the "Temascal"
– a native Mexican sauna.

01 | Between the rustling coco-palms and the
sea, relaxation in beach suite 10.

02 | Not all rooms are quite so balanced in their
design, colors and fabrics as this beach suite.

128 | villa del sol

villa del sol | ixtapa zihuatanejo . mexico

DESIGN: Helmut W. Leins, Enrique Zozaya

The hammock swings gently to and fro, as if in slow motion. And even though you're gazing at the wall of Beach Suite 10, you still have a fabulous view of the ocean. This peculiar scenery, looking out over the private outdoor minipool with its deep blue tiles, is reflected in the sliding glass doors of the room. Even with your back to the beach you can lie up here on the first floor and watch the paragliders drifting across the sky, Mexican families splashing around in the sea and, every

now and then, a beachboy showing off his tricks on the jet ski as if to say, "Hey, look. You could do this too. Just hire the jet ski for a little while – very good price, of course!".

Naturally it would never occur to anyone down on the beach to disturb your tranquillity up here. After all, you are completely incognito, positioned like a good detective. Although this idyllic bay in the former fishing village of Zihuatanejo has developed over the last twenty years –

along with the neighbouring village of Ixtapa – from a tourist no-man's land into a popular resort, it still has that village character and laid-back atmosphere that are missing from Acapulco, 200 kilometers to the south. And even though direct flights link the international airport to the USA, this palm-fringed stretch of coastline is still something of a secret.

The Hotel Villa del Sol has played its role in ensuring the continuing exclusivity of the

place. Or, strictly speaking, its proprietor, Helmut W. Leins, has. When he exchanged his engineering firm in Germany for a plot of Mexican greenery and sandy beach in 1978, all that was here – apart from the towering waves and fine sand – was dense, tropical jungle. "With snakes, scorpions and everything that goes with it", according to Leins, "but also a paradise that takes hold of you and won't let go". So of course you don't really believe him when he tells you that all he

03 04

wanted to do was to kick back and relax, enjoy the pleasures of life and build his little house where he could listen to the eternal sound of the waves. As soon as he arrived in his adoptive home he wasted no time in setting about about his new life as architect, property developer, foreman, organiser and, a few years later, host of the Villa del Sol.

"To begin with there was no water, no electricity and, most importantly, no building workers". So he marched into the village, found himself a few strong-looking men and just told them "You're the bricklayer, you're the joiner and you're the painter". "Fortunately, my engineer's training meant I was able to get my ideas down on paper and explain to everyone exactly what I had in mind". What he had in mind was virtually a small village with some very handsome huts and space for nine bedrooms. "Far too much for my own private use," he decided, and started a second career as hotelier. "Something I'd never dreamed of before". Even today, he prefers to see himself less as a hotelier than as the owner of the property who works away in the background and comes up with the ideas.

And he has plenty of those. Long since honed into an oasis of luxury, the hotel, with its 35 rooms and 35 suites, is a collection of individual designs and tastes which also reflect the history of the hotel.

Not everything can be described as good architecture; some of the rooms are ornate to the point of being kitschy. With all the strong colors, when the sun goes down and the interplay of light and shadow is lost, the atmosphere of a romantic beach hotel quickly disappears. Those seeking an aesthetic experience are therefore recommended to choose one of the beach suites or the new lagoon suites completed at the end of 2002. These are highly individual –

05   06

from the intensely colored and
sumptuously decorated to the
simple and understated. Yet
they all share a sense of
harmony and an ability to
surprise the guest with a fine
selection of furniture, ethnic
accessories and Mexican art.

The blurring of the line between
the indoors and outdoors is
also a recurring element, with
wooden decks or stone patios
and sumptuous foliage. Those
who wish to can surround
themselves with nature. Leins:

"For the Europeans we have
louvre doors and flyscreens, for
the North American guests
glass doors and air conditioning".
The very glass in which the
beach life is so picturesquely
reflected.

03 | The lounge of the Presidential Suite, two floors above the main
restaurant, with a plunge pool just the other side of the white
curtains.

04 | Together with the new building, opened in fall 2002, the Villa
del Sol offers 35 rooms and 35 suites.

05 | The beach suites show, more than other rooms, a mix of ethnic
and minimalist influences.

06 | Wallow in the cool plunge pool, overlooking the beach.

habita | mexico city . mexico

DESIGN: Enrique Norton, Bernardo Gómez-Pimienta, TEN arquitectos

Since its foundation Mexico City has mushroomed in size and is now one of the biggest urban centers in the world with a population of around twenty million. In spite of its vastness and the millions of tons of concrete that sprawl across the landscape, its hilly terrain means that Mexico City still has plenty of green areas, and in winter, snow-covered mountains and volcanoes rise up in the distance, giving an already spectacular location an additional aesthetic touch. Of course, the combination of huge numbers of people and a relatively tight space is always going to raise social issues, but

it is equally a fruitful breeding ground for a vibrant, creative way of life. Given the city's size and potential, it is perhaps surprising that it was not until the Habita opened in 2000 that Mexico City was able to add to its hotel repertoire a boutique property where the emphasis is firmly on design.

Striking even from the outside, the building is in the Polanco quarter right beside Chapultepec Park. In contrast to the often overwhelmingly elaborate architecture found in Mexico City, the Habita, with its almost Zen-like simplicity, is a different kind of work of art. Both the

construction and the interior architecture are by TEN arquitectos whose director is Enrique Norten, Mexico's young star. Their building for Mexico's National History Museum and the National Theater School has already caused something of a sensation. The Habita, which occupies a 1950s apartment block, is an initiative by Rafael Moises, Jaime Micha and Carlos Couturier, the men behind Deseo in Playa del Carmen. TEN arquitectos' most distinctive change to the building was to sheath it with a frosted glass curtain floating free of the original façade which gives the six-story building a

contemporary charisma and a feeling of privacy and seclusion. As the large windows of the rooms also lie behind the wall of ice-blue glass, all disturbances from the outside world are filtered out.

There is a discipline and control about the design of both rooms and furnishings. For people who like refined details, the hotel's architecture is a real treasure trove – in their treatment of the wall intersections and the transitions from one material to another, the designers have taken the art of fugue to a new level. Although sparsely furnished, the rooms are not in

01 | Pool, sundeck and pool bar on the fifth
floor. In the morning, breakfast is served
here, after which the area is turned into
a chilled lounge.

the least unfriendly and, above all else, are extremely practical. The enormous wardrobes have plenty of space for the contents of large suitcases, and clothes do not need to be squeezed onto shelves or into small drawers. The bathrooms are well thought-out, radiating an aesthetic purism. The room design largely dispenses with color. Curtains, walls and bed linen are all completely white. The glass tabletops and wooden and metal chairs are sparingly detailed and seem almost dematerialized. The rooms have a curious feel, in particular, the sight of the building's glass curtain, large

sections of it opaque, creates an atmosphere that seems removed from reality, almost like being in a spaceship. There are just a few transparent slits which afford a view of the neighborhood and its somewhat unattractive buildings.

The roof area, which is spread over two floors, is very much the focal point for life at the hotel. The innovative architecture, of which there has already been more than a suggestion at the reception, in the corridors and in the rooms, is given free rein up here. On the fifth floor, guests seeking relaxation will

find a wooden deck with a small bar and, depending time of day, a breakfast bistro or lounge, as well as a slim swimming pool about 10 meters in length. The sunloungers are in the same dark wood as the flooring and have cushions of pure white. In the middle of the building is the fully glazed fitness room. This may be taking the transparency idea a little too far, for who wants to meet the gaze of the person from the room next door as he is chilling out, relaxing and sipping away at his aperitif, while you are dripping with sweat – and vice versa? By contrast, virtuoso minimalism reigns in the sauna,

04 | 05

02 | The glass skin completely surrounds the
hotel, and acts as a barrier to noise and
other disturbing factors. Only a few
transparent viewing slits allow guests to
peer out at the hotel's neighborhood.

03 | Purism, refined detail, glass and finely
smoothed plaster walls are all typical of the
property's style.

04 | Furnishing in the guestrooms is kept to a
bear minimum, although the atmosphere
remains comfortable, not cold.

05 | The fireplace in the half-open lounge is four
meters long.

06

which is separated from the corridor by a wall of frosted glass, as are the toilets and small washrooms. The same goes for the massage room just next door. Instead of the usual dark, nest-like retreat, this space is bright and cheerful. Light also enters via a narrow gap, from which you can see the outdoor jacuzzi.

After a little sunbathing, a sauna or a spot of treadmill jogging, you can enjoy a drink at the pool bar. Alternatively, one can climb up one floor more to the city's most buzzing bar. Here, dark wooden flooring, exposed concrete, white cushions and glass create a clear, cool atmosphere. The effect of the impressive four-meter hearth is

more functional than cozy, and its design is as rigorously simple as that of the rest of the furnishings. Appropriate lounge music and the opportunity to „see and be seen" are the finishing touches.

07 08

06 | Sauna on the fifth floor. Through a small, narrow opening, one can see the terrace with whirlpool, and the skyscapers in the surrounding area.

07 | The furnishings are mainly created from redwood, steel and glass.

08 | Construction detail of the building's glass wrapper. To the right, the steps lead up to the bar and swimming pool.

ikal del mar | riviera maya . mexiko

DESIGN: Ramiro Alatorre

The stretch of road from Cancun to Tulum on the Mexican Maya Riviera, widened along most of its length to accommodate four lanes of speeding traffic, is a testimony to unbridled optimism. Where, not all that long ago, a bumpy, potholed road wound its way through the coastal scrubland, giant billboards now scream for the attention of passing motorists every hundred meters. Mc Donald's and Kentucky Fried Chicken vie for space, while the children of the passing motorists are exhorted to visit the water park and swim with the dolphins. Most striking of all, however, are the new hotel signs, the boards advertising

land for sale – "60 acres of coastland" – and the developers' boards promising even bigger and more modern shopping centers and hotel complexes. And yet, despite being so clearly geared up for mass tourism, this stretch of coastline between Cancun and Playa del Carmen still has room for the occasional, well-hidden luxury paradise.

One such paradise is "Ikal del Mar", Spanish for "Poetry of the Sea". Anyone heading for this tranquil and seemingly remote jewel needs either extremely detailed directions or a driver who knows where he's going. A taxi driver chosen at random is no guarantee of finding the

place. No wonder; there are deliberately no signs from the highway. About six kilometers north of brash Playa del Carmen is a turning one could easily miss – a dusty gravel track that looks like part of a spaghetti Western set. After another spine-jarring kilometer, civilsation returns. There's a white wall, an abundance of lovingly tended greenery and the logo, elegantly chiselled in stone – a combination of fern, starfish, snail and seagull. Nothing else. No showy sign, no canopy-covered ramp. Instead, the understatement of a private villa and an open reception pavilion. Boardwalks of exotic hardwood, classical

antique furniture, elegantly arranged plants and the welcome breeze of a ceiling fan. The passion for tasteful detail is immediately evident, as is the owners' ability for making guests feel like visiting friends. New arrivals are greeted with refreshing towels, a cocktail and a lengthy chat before being accompanied to their private villa.

The narrow paths to the 29 spacious bohios (bungalows) wind their way between ferns, banana trees, cactii and tropical plants. The luxury huts, each dedicated to a different poet including Neruda, Dario and Alberti, pay homage to the

01 | Only a relatively narrow strip of the grounds has a beach. Although small, it is pristine white and extremely peaceful.

02 | The property's elegant guesthouses are spread across a managed tropical landscape.

01 02

03 04

05

designs and architectural forms of Mayan villages, and yet the end result is far from rustic. It is a sophisticated blend of centuries-old tradition and contemporary comfort with modern technology, which, besides the obligatory air-conditioning, also includes CD, DVD and wide-screen cable TV. Views of the ocean and the island of Cozumel are only available from the Presidential Villa, but oddly enough you'll quickly find you don't mind at all. All the other villas are wonderfully secreted among the tropical jungle in an ambience which, in the northern hemisphere, is usually found only in botanical gardens. The layout of the rooms works particularly well. The living and sleeping area dominates, with dark tropical wood floors and understated, functional furniture which includes a dining table for two, rattan couch, wicker armchairs and home entertainment unit.

The centerpiece of the room is, of course, the bed with its romantic mosquito-net drape. The large windows, all of which have louvre doors to provide shade, bring the outdoors in, as do the two sliding veranda doors. These openings – one glazed and one with just a fly screen for fresh-air fanatics – blur the boundary between the living area and the covered veranda. Every villa has its own private plunge pool, an intimate spot for a nightcap or morning coffee which, incidentally, is left outside your door every morning at whatever time you request. A few mouthfuls and a few laps at the beachside swimming pool in the virginal early-morning is like an instant injection of energy. Guests might then linger by the pool, enjoying the morning. Later, when the sun begins to really burn down, that's when you look forward to retreating to your jungle terrace. Resting on a teak sunlounger with a fat

03 | An unusual range of plantlife makes the grounds seem like a botanical garden.

04 | Reception. Each guest is welcomed as a friend; needless to say, the service is world-class.

05 | Couches draped in mosquito nets, ready for a partner massage in the Mayan Spa.

06 | Beach chairs and sun-loungers in classic wooden designs. From the beach, the view stretches to Cozumel Island.

07 | Wellness treatments are offered in the Mayan Spa, on the beach or even in your own villa. The designers have placed an emphasis on smaller details, such as this basket for hand towels.

08 | Guests can enjoy a massage directly on the beach, under the wafting fabric of this pergola. The temascal sauna hut in the background is less frequently used.

09 | The Azul restaurant on the first floor of the pool and beach building serves fresh fish and seafood.

10 | With just 29 luxurious villas, Ikal del Mar has an exclusive atmosphere. Here, the entire front side of the building can be opened to the terrace and plunge pool.

11 | Whirlpool in the Mayan Spa.

12 | Dressing room in a villa.

13 | The private verandas are well protected by the surrounding greenery.

12 13

novel, lost in your thoughts, breathing in the scent of the tropics – sometimes its difficult to believe that this is real.

The icing on the cake at Ikal del Mar is the unusual spa center. Two circular buildings – one for men, one for women – are cleverly intertwined to form a pretzel shape, housing a sauna, steam bath, candlelit whirlpool and treatment rooms for massage and beauty therapy. The "couples massage" in particular shouldn't be missed. Two beds on a stone platform surrounded by jungle behind the building are shrouded with fine mosquito netting. „We didn't think of that until later", admits the Guest Relations Manager, Abigail, discreetly tending to her guests. „When our masseurs suddenly started doing strange and uncoordinated jigs we wondered what kind of massage they could possibly be giving. We were thinking perhaps it was some ancient Mayan secret, until we noticed it was just the attacking mosquitoes that were causing the strange convulsions!". Making a virtue out of necessity has not only created a wonderful ambience – guests describe it as like being on a floating cloud – but it also looks simply fantastic.

01 | In the center of the corner building, with its 15 rooms and suites, is the lounge. In the daytime, Deseo sweats under the hot sun, but it's a night when the place really comes to life as the hippest address in Playa del Carmen.

deseo | playa del carmen . mexico

DESIGN: Moisés Ison & José Sánchez Manuel Cervantes, Central de Arquitectura

Soft, cream beaches, azur blue sea, beating sun and a gentle ocean breeze – a cliché of relaxation? Certainly, but here there's a difference. In this little town on the Mayan Riviera what's missing is the peace and quiet. In Mexico's latest party capital, Playa del Carmen, feeling good means nightlife, chill-out and more nightlife. Another kind of wellness, not for those looking to sleep all evening and most of the day.

For guests seeking wild, celebrated nights, however, Deseo is just the thing. The creators, Carlos Couturier and brothers, Rafael, Moisés and Jaime Micha, offer chic quarters for cosmopolitan people at Deseo, their second hotel after the Habita in Mexico City. Fifteen rooms and suites are divided over two floors. The cool white spaces, all with marble flooring, are further categorized into balcony and lounge rooms. Lounging in a swinging hammock, guests can choose to have their breakfast brought to them, or simply enjoy a pause to recover from the clubbing the night before.

And the chances are, the night before started off at the hotel's lounge, where selected DJ's kick the party off. Later, the Deseo scene moves on to local bars and restaurants such as „Ula Gula", „Apasionado" or „Cuba". The guys behind the decks give guests the best tips on where's hot and where's not.

Designed by the young Mexican architectural team, Central de Arquitectura, Deseo first opened its doors in October 2001, and blends modern and surprisingly traditional elements. Low folding stools and bedside tables made of teak leave a classic Mexican impression. Balcony railings from Mangle tree branches, set against the straight-lined, stark white architecture of the main building form a clear example of the mix on show. A glance at the arcades around the courtyard deck creates a direct link to the creativity of the architects. Features appear as if drawn on a sheet of paper in thick, soft graphite lines.

02   03

From the beginning on, the creative team laid emphasis on their concept of "stylish easy living", and the result is a corresponding one. Whether summer or winter, Deseo (also a member of the design hotels™ group) is a center for young club scenesters lounging under the Mexican sun. The beach is just two minutes from the hotel, but for many guests the pool offers a more attractive and convenient alternative. Here, the bronzed bodies flop down on cushioned daybeds, framed by hanging linen sheets that ripple lazily in the wind. But days at Deseo normally start on the lounge deck, with a Euro-Latin breakfast of fresh juices and fruits. Later in the day and in the evening, as the music gets turned up, an array of tapas is also served at the central bar.

When guests retire to their rooms, they can continue to experience the live DJ's – the doors are unfortunately poorly isolated and let the bass tones through. Help is, however, on hand in the bedside table drawer. Alongside a small box with condoms sits the answer: a pair of earplugs.

02 | Only suites have freestanding bath-tubs.

03 | Contemporary design with historical influences. The buildings and furniture both reflect the aesthetic innovations of central de arquitectura.

04 | The steps which lead from Fifth Avenue to the lounge at Deseo mimic the construction of a Mayan temple. The reception is to the right.

05 | The design embraces concepts of functionality and simplicity, with few materials and straight lines. Here, the reception.

06 | Dramatically framed daybeds catch the eye. At night, these form part of the relaxed club atmosphere. In the background are guestrooms, separated from the public areas only by opaque glazing. Those trying to sleep before 1am will need earplugs.

chile

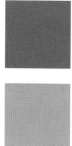

explora en atacama | san pedro de atacama . chile

DESIGN: German del Sol

With a relative humidity of two percent or less, the Atacama Desert in northern Chile is one of the driest places on earth. Somewhat of a challenge for hotel constructors, one might think. It is precisely this climatic extreme that gave German del Sol the added impetus to install a counterpiece to his other property, explora en Patagonia. Just as their natural backdrops differ, so do the two hotels.

The explora en Atacama is situated 8,000 feet above sea level and resembles a futuristic fort. At present, the hotel boasts 50 guestrooms set within the elongated, enclosed wings of the structure and arranged in the form of a parallelogram around the main building, which also contains a lobby, gallery, restaurant and business offices. Center-hung roofs shaped like airplane wings protrude a full 10 feet over the building and protect the terraces below from the sun and wind. In keeping with local design tradition, the rooms at the Atacama are small – most social or commercial life in the region takes place outdoors, encouraged by average daytime temperatures of around 75 °F. At the resort, this natural lifestyle is adhered to, and emphasis is laid on the exploration of the nearly limitless surroundings, either on foot, on horseback or on mountain bike. Guided groups of eight or less are taken by the hotel's local ranger into the wide expanse of the desert and steppe landscape, up among the Andean peaks, volcanoes and geysers, or to numerous Inca and Tiahuaniaco ruins. A comprehensive irrigation system developed by the area's original inhabitants is still used today for local agriculture and also supplies water to the hotel. Seizing upon this pre-existing technology, German del Sol set canals, waterfalls and pools throughout the resort. As with the irrigation systems, the resulting creations appear as man-made but harmonious components of the landscape.

Architectural, social and economical integration, are crucial factors in the philosophy of the explora hotels. Local villages produce the raw ingredients used in the hotel's kitchen, local artisans provided their skills in the furnishing and construction of the hotel and local artists display their works at the property.

Such an immersion in the indigenous culture can be an overwhelming experience for guests, but it's an experience that can open up new ways of thinking about the world, and helps visitors to explora en Atacama discover something new about themselves.

01 | Luxurious baracks in the Atacama Desert, 2440 meters above sea level. The nearest airport is around 100 km away.

02 | German del Sol has masterfully blended and controlled sunlight, color and materials.

03 | The volcanic foothills of the Andes offer fascinating, ever-changing locations to explore.

04 | Almost like a monument: WC and changing room building by the pool.

05 | White plaster walls, stone floors and wooden decks create a snug ambience.

06 | 07 The furniture and objets d'art have all been produced by local craftsmen.

explora en patagonia | torres del paine . chile

DESIGN: German del Sol

It takes a good six hours to drive from the nearest airport in Punta Arenas, the southern-most city on the globe, to the hotel explora en Patagonia. But the trip to the end of the world is made infinitely easier by the majestic natural backdrop of the Torres del Paine national park on the southern tip of Chile. Located above the 50th parallel, the Torres del Paine is a UNESCO world biosphere reserve. Here, in this thinly settled and mostly pristine example of Patagonian landscape, Chilean architect German del Sol set about creating an ecologically-friendly hotel project. It's a theme that comes naturally to del Sol,

who is also the founder of the Explora travel agency, a body dedicated to operating sustainable tourism ventures throughout South America.

On the banks of Lake Pahoe, this luxury hotel is framed by steep, generally snow-covered mountains reaching 14,000 feet in height; a perfect starting point for modest explorations. Using a geometry usually found in cities, del Sol has attempted to create a counterpoint to the flowing natural forms around. Nonetheless, the property betrays the limited effect that architecture can achieve, regardless of talent and

creativity, when dwarfed by such impressive natural environments. Even though the angles and slopes clearly indicate the pencil lines and strokes of a gifted planner, the white-encrusted building looks from afar like a layer of snow before the thaw.

Viewed from up close, however, the hotel springs forth like an observation station with a five-star ambiance. Its nature lodge contains a mere 30 rooms, each one uniquely designed. Lighting, furniture and accessories, all were designed by del Sol and manufactured by local artisans using materials native to the region. Many of

the rooms boast panoramic views of nearby waterfalls, mountains, glaciers or lakes.

Every guestroom comes equipped with all of the creature comforts one could reasonably expect. With so much awe-inspiring nature around, the television is a fairly surprising addition and one that usually remains untouched. Instead, after a day's trekking, most guests prefer to relax with a sauna or massage, then savor some of the excellent cuisine on offer, accompanied, of course, by a glass or two of Chilean Chardonnay or Cabernet Sauvignon.

01 | Giant natural backdrops at the end of the world. The explora hotel is the only luxury resort in the whole of the Torres del Paine National Park, at Chile's southern tip.

02 | Gourmet restaurant with local and international flavors and magnificent views on Torres del Paine National Park

03 | Despite the geometrically clear lines and reduced furnishings, the hotel's interiors are warm and balanced.

04 | Views of the mountains can even be enjoyed from the bathrooms...

05 | ...or in bed. Use of the natural scenery is a basic element of the whole property's design concept.

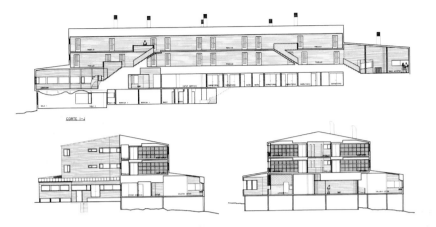

06

CORTE I-J

06 | Indoor swimming pool with a view of Lake Pahoe and the mountains of the national park. The open-air, wooden deck is the location for a whirlpool.

07 | Side and interiors projections of the building.

08 | Wood is also the main material in the hotel's interiors. The cladding effect in this rooms makes it optically longer.

09 | An example of the natural style of decoration prevalent throughout the hotel.

08 09

hotel summary

Country / Location	Address	Information	Architecture & Design	Page
USA Healdsburg, CA	Hotel Healdsburg 25 Matheson Street Healdsburg, CA 95448 USA www.hotelhealdsburg.com www.designhotels.com	opened 2001 55 spacious rooms and suites garden, pool, spa bar, wine-tasting room, Dry Creek Restaurant, in the middle of Healdsburg, Sonoma County, 70 miles north of San Francisco	Frost Tsuji Architects David Baker & Associates	12
USA Big Sur, CA	Post Ranch Inn Highway 1 Big Sur, CA 93920 USA www.postranchinn.com	opened 1992 30 guestrooms in mountain, coast, ocean and tree houses Sierra Mar Restaurant, library, boutique, hiking trail, infinity pool, fitness center, spa facilities, yoga, shiatsu, reiki located on a cliff above Big Sur, 30 min. south of Monterey and 2 hrs. south of San José (intl. airports)	Mickey Meunning Janet Gay Freed	18
USA Santa Barbara, CA	Bacara Resort & Spa 8301 Hollister Avenue Santa Barbara, CA 93117 USA www.bacararesort.com	opened 2000 311 rooms and 49 suites Spa Café, The Bistro and gourmet restaurant Miró spacious spa facilities with beauty saloon, sauna, steambath, pools, direct beach access, conference center, golf course 15 min. north of Santa Barbara	Hill Architects Glazier Architects Gary Beggs Perdian Int. Landscape Architects	22
USA Desert Hot Springs, CA	Hope Springs 68075 Club Circle Drive Desert Hot Springs, CA 92240 USA www.hopespringsresort.com	opened 1999 10 rooms, some with kitchenette self-service kitchen, lounge and living room, pools with hot spring water, massage menu library with large variety of CDs and books 15 min. north of Palm Springs	Steve & Misako Samiof Mike Haggerty	28
USA Desert Hot Springs, CA	Miracle Manor 12589 Reposo Way Desert Hot Springs, CA 92240 USA www.miraclemanor.com	opened 1997 6 rooms, some with kitchenette, lounge with self-service kitchen pools with hot spring water, small spa facilities 15 min. north of Palm Springs	April Greiman Michael Rotondi	32

Country / Location	Address	Information	Architecture & Design	Page
USA Desert Hot Springs, CA	Sagewater Spa 12697 Eliseo Road Desert Hot Springs, CA 92240 USA www.sagewaterspa.com	opened 2001 7 rooms, some with kitchenette patio, poolside barbecue and DSL internet access pools with hot spring water, massage menu 15 min. north of Palm Springs	Rhoni Epstein Cristina Pestana	36
USA Sedona, AZ	Enchantment Resort & Mii amo Spa 525 Boynton Canyon Road Sedona, AZ 86336 USA www.miiamo.com	opened 2001 Enchantment Resort has 220 rooms, Mii amo 14 rooms and 2 suites, Yavapai Restaurant, Mii amo Spa Café, Tii Gavo Lounge, Mii amo Spa offers 3, 4 and 7 night all-inclusive programs, 1.5 hrs. north of Phoenix	Gluckman Mayner Architects Dana Tang Greg Yang	42
USA Dolores, CO	Dunton Hot Springs 52068 West Fork Rd. #38 Dolores, CO 81323 USA www.duntonhotsprings.com	opened 2001 former gold-digger village 12 timber houses and wigwam tent, total of 24 guests indoor pools with hot spring water, spa treatments, restaurant with local specialities 50 miles north of Dolores, Colorado	George Greenbank Katrin Henkel Bernt Kuhlmann	48
USA Jackson Hole, WY	Amangani 1535 North East Butte Road Jackson Hole, WY 83001 USA www.amangani.com	opened 1999 29 suites, 8 deluxe suites and 3 top suites, each of them with bathroom and fireplace in the living room bar, lounge and restaurant, library, pool and whirlpool, fitness rooms, various outdoor facilities near the popular Yellowstone National Park	Edward Tuttle	52
USA Miami Beach, FL	The Shore Club 1901 Collins Avenue Miami Beach, FL 33139 USA www.shoreclub.com	opened 2002 325 rooms, 70 suites, penthouse, 8 two-story pool cabanas, Nobu's Restaurant and Lounge, terrace restaurant, pool bar Suñdari Spa and beauty saloon, direct beach access in the center of South Beach	David Chipperfield	56

hotel summary

Country / Location	Address	Information	Architecture & Design	Page
USA Miami Beach, FL	Beach House Bal Harbour 9449 Collins Avenue Miami Beach, FL 33139 USA www.rubellhotels.com	opened 1999 165 guestrooms and suites Atlantic Restaurant und Seahorse Bar, poolside wellness cabanas, pool, gym, direct beach access 20 min. from South Beach 40 min. from Miami International Airport	Scott Sanders Ralph Lauren Group	62
Turks & Caicos Providenciales	Parrot Cay P.O. Box 164 Providenciales Turks & Caicos Islands www.parrot-cay.com	opened 1999 60 guestrooms and suites, some with plunge pool Lotus and terrace restaurant, special spa kitchen tennis courts, gym, scuba diving, golf course Shambala Spa 1 hr. flight from Miami	Keith Hobbs	66
Puerto Rico San Juan	Water Club 2 Tartak Street Isla Verde, Carolina Puerto Rico 00979 www.waterclubsanjuan.com www.designhotels.com	opened 2001 84 rooms and suites, most with ocean-view restaurant, Liquid Bar, Wet Bar roof-top sundeck and pool, spa facilities, gym in the basement located on the beach in Isla Verde	Annie Falgas Pedro Rosario Designworks	70
British Virgin Islands Virgin Gorda	Katitche Point Greathouse Plum Bay Road The Valley British Virgin Islands www.katitchepoint.com	opened 2001 4 rooms and 1 master suite professional kitchen, poolside barbecue, chef upon request 3 different beaches within 5 minutes walking distance 30 min. by ferry from airport Tortola, Beef Island	Michael Helm	74
Anguilla Maunday's Bay	Cap Juluca P.O. Box 240 Maunday's Bay Anguilla www.capjuluca.com	opened 1998 58 rooms und junior suites, 7 suites, 6 pool villas George's, Kemia and Pimm's Restaurant various sports activities, windsurfing, sailing, scuba diving holistic spa treatments, new spa center opening 2003	Oskar Farmer Bob Perkins Xanadu	78

Country / Location		Address	Information	Architecture & Design	Page
Antigua & Barbuda	Barbuda	K-Club Barbuda, West Indies www.designhotels.com	opened 2000 35 rooms, 5 lodge rooms and 1 garden villa restaurant and bar 9-hole golf course	Mariuccia Mandelli Gianni Gamondi	82
Barbados	Paynes Bay	The House Paynes Bay St James Barbados www.eleganthotels.com/thehouse	opened 2001 31 suites Daphne's Barbados, gourmet restaurant children from 12 years permitted	Luciano Colombo	84
Grenada	Morne Rouge Bay	Laluna P.O. Box 1500 Morne Rouge Bay Grenada www.laluna.com www.designhotels.com	opened 2001 16 cottages with private plunge pools and private terrace restaurant "La Luna Kitchen" with fine selection of wines, bar and open-air lounge CD and video library 10 min. from international airport	Carmelina Santoro Gabriella Giuntolli	88
Curaçao	Piscaderabay	Floris Suite Hotel P.O. Box 6246 Piscaderabay, Curaçao Dutch Caribbean www.florissuitehotel.com www.designhotels.com	opened 2001 40 junior suites, 32 royal suites Sjalotte and La Plage Hook's Hut bar and restaurant 10 min. from Willemstad	Jan des Bouvrie	94
Mexico	Puerto Vallarta	Verana Casa Carocol Calle Cuanhtemoc 557 Puerto Vallarta, Jalisco 48300 Mexico www.verana.com	opened 2000 6 individually designed buildings dinner menu, bar, pool, library, jungle spa in a secluded bay approx. 1.5 hrs. south of Puerto Vallarta, final approach by boat	Heinz Legler Veronique Lièvre	100

hotel summary

Country / Location		Address	Information	Architecture & Design	Page
Mexico	Puerto Vallarta	Hotelito Desconocido Carretera a Mismaloya 479-102 Puerto Vallarta, Jalisco 48380 Mexico www.hotelito.com	opened 1996 21 buildings on stilts and 9 beach bungalows pool bar, restaurant secluded sand beach, horse riding 1.5 hrs. drive south of Puerto Vallarta	Marcello Murzilli	106
Mexico	Costalegre	Casas de Careyes P.O. Box 87 Melaque, Jalisco 48980, Mexico www.careyes.com.mx www.mexicoboutiquehotels.com	opened 1972 42 villas, from single room appartment up to a house with 8 rooms, leisure village Casitas de Las Flores beach restaurant Playa Rosa, polo club 2 hrs. south of Puerto Vallarta, 1 hr. north of Manzanillo	Marco Aldaco Diego Villaseñor Jean Claude Galibert	112
Mexico	Costalegre	El Careyes Km. 53,5 Carretera Barra de Navidad – Puerto Vallarta, Costa Carreyes, Jalisco 48970 , Mexico www.mexicoboutiquehotels.com www.starwood.com	opened 1993 48 guestrooms and suites, terrace restaurant and bar with sea-view, conference center for up to 20 people, pool and private beach, spa facilities, gym, tennis courts 2 hrs. south of Puerto Vallarta, 1 hr. north of Manzanillo	Diego Villaseñor Grupo Plan	118
Mexico	Cihuatlán	El Tamarindo Km. 7,5 Carretera Melaque – Puerto Vallarta, Cihuatlán, Jalisco 48970, Mexico www.mexicoboutiquehotels.com www.starwood.com	opened 1997 28 villas with private plunge pool or jacuzzi, terrace restaurant on different levels with seá-view pool, spa, temascal, jungle gym, 18-hole golf course, tennis courts, conference center for up to 60 people 2.5 hrs. south of Puerto Vallarta, 45 min. north of Manzanillo	Luis Bosoms Grupo Plan	122
Mexico	Ixtapa / Zihuatanejo	Villa del Sol Playa la Ropa, P.O. Box 84 Ixtapa Zihuatanejo 40880, Mexico www.hotelvilladelsol.net www.mexicoboutiquehotels.com	opened 1982 35 rooms and 35 suites (garden, lagoon or beach), some with plunge pools gourmet restaurant Villa del Sol, Cantina bar and grill direct beach access, various pools 15 min. from international airport Ixtapa-Zihuatanejo	Helmut W. Leins Enrique Zozaya	128

Country / Location		Address	Information	Architecture & Design	Page
Mexico	Mexico City	Habita Av. Presidente Masaryk 201, Colonia Polanco, Mexico D.F. 11560, Mexico www.hotelhabita.com www.designhotels.com	opened 2000 32 rooms and 4 suites restaurant Aura, Area bar and roof-top terrace conference center with internet access roof-top terrace with pool, gym, sauna, steambath, massage located in Polanco quarter, approx. 30 min. from airport	Enrique Norten Bernardo Gómez-Pimienta TEN arquitectos	132
Mexico	Riviera Maya	Ikal del Mar Villa Resort & Spa Playa Xcalacoco, Riviera Maya, Quintana Roo 77710, Mexico www.ikaldelmar.com www.slh.com	opened 2002 29 villas with private terraces, garden and plunge pools restaurant, beach bar Mayan spa with temascal direct beach access 40 min. from Cancun International Airport	Ramiro Alatorre	138
Mexico	Playa del Carmen	Deseo 5th Ave. & 12th St. Playa del Carmen 77710, Mexico www.hoteldeseo.com www.designhotels.com	opened 2001 15 rooms and suites lounge deck with bar, music until 1 a.m. self-service kitchen and lounge pool, sun deck – 5 min. to beach in the center of Playa del Carmen	Moisés Ison José Sánchez Manuel Cervantes Central de Arquitectura	144
Chile	San Pedro de Atacama	explora en Atacama Av. Américo Vespucio Sur 80, Piso 5, Santiago, Chile www.explora-chile.com	opened 1998 50 rooms and suites restaurant with regional cuisine various pools, wellness center art gallery and lobby located 2,500 m above sea level in the Atacama desert	German del Sol	150
Chile	Torres del Paine	explora en Patagonia Av. Américo Vespucio Sur 80, Piso 5, Santiago, Chile www.explora-chile.com	opened 1993 30 rooms restaurant, bar and library indoor pool, jacuzzi, gym and massage private moorings on the lake located at Lake Pahoe in the Torres del Paine National Park	German del Sol	154

architects & designers

Name	Hotel	Page
Ramiro Alatorre	Ikal del Mar	138
Marco Aldaco	Casas de Careyes	112
David Baker & Associates	Hotel Healdsburg	12
Gary Beggs	Bacara Resort & Spa	22
Luis Bosoms	El Tamarindo	122
Jan des Bouvrie	Floris Suite Hotel	94
Gian Franco Brignone	Casas de Careyes	112
Central de Arquitectura	Deseo	144
Manuel Cervantes	Deseo	144
David Chipperfield	The Shore Club	56
Luciano Colombo	The House	84
Designworks	Water Club	70
Rhoni Epstein	Sagewater Spa	36
Annie Falgas	Water Club	70
Oskar Farmer	Cap Juluca	78
Janet Gay Freed	Post Ranch Inn	18
Frost Tsuji Architects	Hotel Healdsburg	12
Jean Claude Galibert	Casas de Careyes	112
Gianni Gamondi	K-Club	82
Gabriella Giuntolli	Laluna	88
Glazier Architects	Bacara Resort & Spa	22
Gluckman Mayner Architects	Enchantment Resort &	42
	Mii amo Spa	
Bernardo Gómez-Pimienta	Habita	132
George Greenbank	Dunton Hot Springs	48
April Greiman	Miracle Manor	32
Grupo Plan	El Tamarindo	122
Mike Haggerty	Hope Springs	28
Michael Helm	Katitche Point Greathouse	74
Katrin Henkel	Dunton Hot Springs	48
Hill Architects	Bacara Resort & Spa	22
Keith Hobbs	Parrot Cay	66
Moisés Ison	Deseo	44
Bernt Kuhlmann	Dunton Hot Springs	48
Ralph Lauren Group	Beach House Bal Harbor	62
Heinz Legler	Verana	100

Name	Hotel	Page
Helmut W. Leins	Villa del Sol	128
Veronique Lièvre	Verana	100
Mariuccia Mandelli	K-Club	82
Mickey Meunning	Post Ranch Inn	18
Marcello Murzilli	Hotelito Desconocido	106
Enrique Norten	Habita	132
Perdian Int. Landscape Arch.	Bacara Resort & Spa	22
Bob Perkins	Cap Juluca	78
Cristina Pestana	Sagewater Spa	36
Pedro Rosario	Water Club	70
Michael Rotondi	Miracle Manor	32
Steve & Misako Samiof	Hope Springs	28
José Sánchez	Deseo	144
Scott Sanders	Beach House Bal Harbor	62
Carmelina Santoro	Laluna	88
German del Sol	Explora en Atacama	150
	Explora en Patagonia	154
Dana Tang	Enchantment Resort &	42
	Mii amo Spa	
TEN arquitectos	Habita	132
Edward Tuttle	Amangani	52
Diego Villaseñor	Casas de Careyes	112
	El Careyes	118
Xanadu	Cap Juluca	78
Greg Yang	Enchantment Resort &	42
	Mii amo Spa	
Enrique Zozaya	Villa del Sol	128

photo credits

Name	Hotel	Page (Photos)
Archive Amanresorts	Amangani	52 (all)
Rainer Baumann		10, 64, 98
Will Blanchard	Dunton Hot Springs	48,161
Klaus Brechenmacher		10, 64, 98
Sofia Brignone	Casas de Careyes	112 (2, 4-11), 164
Archive El Careyes	El Careyes	164
Marcelo Cuelho	Sagewater Spa	36 (1,3,4,5,7), 161
Archive Eleganthotels	The House	4 (all), 163
Archive Explora	Explora en Atacama	148, 150 (all), 165
	Explora en Patagonia	154 (all), 165
Francine Fleischer	Parrot Cay	66 (all), 162
Archive Floris Suite Hotel	Floris Suite Hotel	94 (all), 165
Michael Helm	Katitche Point	74 (sketch)
Archive Habita	Habita	32 (sig., 1-5, 7)
Archive Katitche Point	Katitche Point	74 (sig., 2,4)
Archive Krizia	K-Club	82 (all), 163
Archive Laluna	Laluna	88 (sig., 1, 5-8)
Archive lebensart		Cover (sig.)
Phil Lauro	Dunton Hot Springs	48
Heinz Legler	Verana	100 (all), 162
		Backcover, 4 (1, 8)
Batista Moon	Post Ranch Inn	18
Undine Pröhl	Deseo	144 (all), 165
		Cover, 4 (3)
Jack Richmond	Dunton Hot Springs	48
Archive Rubell Hotels	Beach House	62 (all)
Fritz v.d. Schulenburg	Dunton Hot Springs	48
Polina Sirosh	Enchantment Resort &	42 (2)
	Mii amo Spa	
Archive The Shore Club	The Shore Club	56 (1), 161
Patrick Tregenza	Post Ranch Inn	18, 160
Archive Villa del Sol	Villa del Sol	164
Harry Zernike	Enchantment Resort &	42 (1,4,5,7,8)
	Mii amo Spa	9 (13)

all other photos by: Martin Nicholas Kunz

imprint

Bibliographic information published by Die Deutsche Bibliothek
Die Deutsche Bibliothek lists this publication in the Deutsche
Nationalbibliografie; detailed bibliographic data are available in
the Internet at http://dnb.ddb.de

ISBN 3-929638-87-8

lebensart global networks AG
Konrad-Adenauer-Allee 35 I 86150 Augsburg I Germany
p +49-821-34545928 I f +49-821-34545925
http://www.lebensart-ag.com I publishing@lebensart-ag.com

avedition GmbH
Königsallee 57 I 71638 Ludwigsburg I Germany
p +49-7141-1477391 I f +49-7141-1477399
http://www.avedition.de I info@avedition.de

Publisher   I Martin Nicholas Kunz
Translations / Editing   I Scott M. Crouch, Nigel Geens (Lingserve)
Texts (page) I Ursula Dietmair (62, 94); Riva Medien, Frank
Bantle / Heinfried Tacke (48, 52, 66, 82, 84, 100, 144);
Ina Sinterhauf (132); Martin Nicholas Kunz (all other texts)
Research   I Hanna Martin, Saskia Lang, Scott M. Crouch,
Art Direction   I Willem Krauss, Michael Schickinger
Production   I Markus Hartmann, Martina Weißer, Hanna Martin
Printing I Vorarlberger Verlagsanstalt AG, Dornbirn

Special Thanks to: Heidi van Acker, Floris Suite Hotel I Frank
Bantle, Riva Medien I Bernardo Bertucci, Laluna I Sofia Brignone,
Giorgio Brignone, Casas de Careyes I Sheri Broedlow, Bacara
Resort I Trina Dingler-Ebert, Amanresorts I Rhoni Epstein,
Sagewater Spa I Fernanda Gembe, Hotelito Desconocido I April
Greiman, Miracle Manor I Eustace „Guish" Guishard, Cap Juluca I
Christoph Henkel, Dunton Hot Springs I Sophie Hennell,
Columbus PRCo I Regine & Christian Hodeige I Charles Hossle,
Laluna I John Hunt, Bacara Resort I Reto Kade, El Tamarindo I
Mariuccia Mandelli, K-Club I Teresa Keller-Rabe, Water Club I
Bernt Kuhlmann, Dunton Hot Springs I Nina Kumana,
Amanresorts I David Kurland, Water Club I Heinz Legler, Verana I
Helmut W. Leins, Villa del Sol I Leyla Marchetto, Paul Wilmot
Communications I Lucy Mart, Elegant Hotels I Moisés Micha,
Deseo & Habita I Marcello Murzilli, Hotelito Desconocido I Alexa
Hokanson, Enchantment Resort & Mii Amo Spa I Cristina Pestana,
Sagewater Spa I Aldo Pinto, K-Club I Victoria L.Pratt, Mexico
Boutique Hotels I Dan Priano, Post Ranch Inn I Rui Reis, The
Luxury Collection – Starwood I Sonia Rendigs I Abigail Rivera,
Ikal del Mar I Encarnita Rivera, Gluckman Mayner Architects I
Michael Rotondi, Miracle Manor I Jennifer Rubell, Beach House
Bal Harbour I Steve & Misako Samiof, Hope Springs I Circe
Sher, Hotel Healdsburg I German del Sol, Explora I April Whann,
El Tamarindo I Bea Wolfe, Passport Resorts I Harry Zernike I
Maamke van Zwol, Floris Suite Hotel

design hotels™, www.designhotels.com
Mexico Boutique Hotels, www.mexicoboutiquehotels.com

Scott Michael Crouch

Martin Nicholas Kunz

Born 1976 in Southampton,
England. Scott completed his
degree in law at the London
School of Economics in 1997,
before taking the sideways
step into tourism and
communications. Now based in
Augsburg, Germany, following
two years in Spain, Scott is
co-editor of the entire
"best designed…" series.

Born 1957 in Hollywood.
Martin is Senior Vice
President publishing and
communications of lebensart
global networks AG. Martin
worked as an editor for
several German and other
international magazines such
as "design report" and was
Managing Director of New
Media for the German
publisher DVA, a company
known for its architecture,
design and craft books,
magazines and web sites.
He is author and co-author
of several design, craft and
construction books, and
since 2001, author and
publisher of the avedition
lebensart book series "best
designed…"; six books of the
world's most beautiful hotels.